First published in the United Kingdom
Branded Content Marketing Association

The Stylus Building,
116 Old Street,
London EC1V 9BG

www.thebcma.info

BCMA is a registered company in the United Kingdom, number: 07609220

© Branded Content Marketing Association (BCMA)

Twenty Years, Another Branded Content Story © Branded Content Marketing Association (BCMA)

Author: Andrew Canter
Editor: Greg Turzynski

All rights reserved. No part of this publication may be reproduced, stored in a retrieval system, or transmitted, in any form or by any means, electronic, mechanical, photocopying, recording or otherwise, without the prior written permission of the Branded Content Marketing Association (BCMA).

ISBN: 9798359063395

For all of the incredibly talented creators of amazing branded content and influencer marketing

Dear Christine
Welcome aboard!
Best wishes
Andrew

"In anything at all, perfection is finally attained not when there is no longer anything to add, but when there is no longer anything to take away, when a body has been stripped down to its nakedness."

Yvon Chouinard, Founder, Patagonia

Twenty Years, Another Branded Content Story

CONTENTS

	Page
PREFACE: Andrew Canter	7
FOREWORD: Sir John Hegarty	12

CONTRIBUTING EXPERTS:

Professor Jonathan Hardy – *Rules And Guidance Needed To Grow Responsible Branded Content Marketing*	14
Dr. Helen Powell – *Are We There Yet? The Temporal Dynamics of Motoring Branded Content*	18
Maya Bogle – *Can Purpose-Led Brands Deliver Better Results?*	22
Gordon Glenister – *The Rise And Rise Of Influencer Marketing*	25
Simon Orpin – *Drive To Thrive*	31
Jeanette Okwu – *Brand Storytelling Takes Centre-Stage*	34
Simon Bell – *What The Changing Business Models In Streaming Tell Us About The Future Of Branded Content*	36
Shannon Walker – *The Evolution Of Creativity To Disrupt Change*	41
Spero Patricios – *Doing Good: Achieving Growth With Branded Content*	45
Lawrence Ribero – *Take The Risk*	48
Karnvir Mundrey – *Navigating The Indian Content Marketing Jungle*	50
Dr. Sevil Yesiloglu – *Future Trends Of Influencer Marketing: Virtual Versus In-House*	53
Haem Roy – *Here, There And Everywhere*	56
Daniel Sánchez – *Does Your Brand Have What It Takes To Make An Authentic Connection?*	58
Álvaro Bermúdez de Castro – *Content With Purpose*	63
Adam Kaczmarski – *The Power of Branded Content Production*	66
Professor Iain Macrury – *Branded Content And Long-Form Semiotics: The Case Of Snackmasters*	73
Silvia Velasco Praga – *Metaverse And The Future Of Branded Content*	84
Olgierd Cygan – *The Real Branded Content*	86
Mariana Lorena – *Brand Content: Effectively Effective. How To?*	88
Armando Díaz – *The Mind & Heart for Everlasting Content*	90
Chantal Rickards OBE – *Think Different*	92
Greg Turzynski – *It's Time To Get Noticed*	94
Jo Farmer, Geraint Lloyd-Taylor, Alan Hunt & Emily Stirling – *Influencing Your Relationship: Key Points For Brands To Consider When Contracting With An Influencer*	99
Nina Glynn – *Ad Blockers, Advertisement, And Advocacy: Why Gen-Z Is Blocking Paid Ads In Favour Of Real Voices*	103

CONTENTS

	Page
CONTRIBUTING EXPERTS:	
Melanie Loeper & Megan Tandy – *What Branded Content Campaigns Can Learn From Sports Sponsorship Data Analysis*	111
Stefano Marrone – *Why Animation Is The Best Way To Campaign About Sensitive Topics*	115
Sandra Freisinger-Heinl & Christina Kufer – *Green Advertising And Content In Germany*	121
Patricia Weiss – *Brand Storytelling And Branded Content: The Powerful Meeting Between People's Truth And The Brand's Truth*	131
James Hayr – *Brand Building Content*	134
Sandra Lehner – *The Future Of Luxury Is Web3*	137
Martin Laing – *Converging Storylines*	142
Tom Higgins – *How Gifting Became An Inflection Point For Brand Storytelling*	148
Dr Tauheed A. Ramjaun – *Fighting Branded Misinformation*	151
Monique Centrone Ph.D. – *Making Sense Of NFTs*	154
Rick Parkhill – *Brand Storytelling – A Perfect Storm*	162
Sylvia Enotiades – *The Evolution Of Influencer Marketing*	167
Jessica Millowick – *Making A Market That Works For Talent And Brands*	171
Dr Rula Al Abdulrazak – *Is Branded Content Capable Of Increasing A Brand's Inclusivity?*	175
Rebecca Allen – *Harnessing The Voice Of Your Customer*	179
Julie Dardour – *Content Lover: A Life Of Passion*	182
Adam Harris – *How Do You Do, Fellow Marketers*	184
Katherine Elizabeth Ekrami – *Is It On Purpose?*	189
Emily Bull – *The Time Is Right For Branded Video Content*	194
Adam Smith – *From Industry to Higher Education*	197
Cristian Liarte – *Branded Content Evolution: Brand Influence*	200
Patrick Lindon – *The Year Of Influencer Marketing...I Mean Rabbit*	201
Bruce Bildsten – *BMW Films: Perfect Mini Movies*	205
ACKNOWLEDGEMENTS	209
ABOUT THE AUTHOR	210
ABOUT THE BRANDED CONTENT MARKETING ASSOCIATION	211
DISCLAIMER	212

PREFACE
by Andrew Canter

It's been a fascinating five years since we last brought the branded content thought-leaders together to share their views on the past, present, and future of the industry. This was a particularly seminal moment as we rapidly moved towards the 'age of influencer marketing' which has changed the global communications landscape forever.

Having worked in the branded content industry for twenty-five years, I have been involved with and witnessed many wonderful examples of creativity at the highest level. As the head of a global branded content member association, I have also had the privilege of judging the best work from across the globe. I have met many truly inspiring and visionary branded content practitioners. It strikes me that we have one thing in common – we are all hugely passionate about producing great branded content.

I am extremely proud to lead an organisation that has been at the forefront of branded content for the past twenty-years and the incredible progress that has been made during that period. Over the years, we have seen extraordinary examples of branded content creativity from major brands, such as, Red Bull, Lego, BMW, Chipotle, Unilever, Procter & Gamble and Nike, to name a few.

It is worthwhile taking a moment to celebrate the stand out achievements of Red Bull as a branded content pioneer who have continued to invest smartly in funding their own outstanding content, including Felix Baumgartner's jump from outer space. The creation of the Red Bull Media House was a game-changer, that inspires beyond ordinary stories, cementing their place as the leader in producing incredibly entertaining branded content.

With the rapid growth of influencers and content creators, we took the decision to use our knowledge and learning from branded content to focus on professionalising influencer marketing by launching a dedicated global chapter. We have seen the rise of hugely 'influential' creators becoming brands within their own right, such as, Elon Musk, Kendall Jenner, KSI, Jay-Z, PewDiePie and MrBeast. The new chapter has helped brands navigate the challenges this often-complex sector brings.

PREFACE

Another area of great potential has been the continued advancement of technology. It is always difficult to predict how this will impact on the future of the branded content industry. One of the greatest quotes about technology was by Thomas Watson, CEO of IBM. In 1943, Watson said, *"I think there is a world market for maybe five computers."*

Taking this into account, I always say the one thing that is guaranteed about predicting the future is that you are going to be wrong; but it's to what degree you get it wrong that counts!

However, what we do know is that billions of people own smartphones or smart devices and generally consume their content on the move and 'on demand' which will continue to grow. Many brands are added to their customer's experience through enhanced applications using Augmented Reality (AR). Great examples of brands using this technology are Nintendo's Pokémon Go App, IKEA's Mobile App, L'Oréal's Make-Up App and Google's Star Wars Stickers. This has also been effective in enabling people to 'try before they buy' online.

The other technological advancement we have seen is in branded Virtual Reality (VR) experiences. One of the key challenges with VR, is the additional cost of the headset, however, these have been reducing over time. The rich experience that VR can add to branded content can be extraordinary. A good example is allowing potential car buyers to 'test drive' a car without going anywhere. Another excellent example was the Merrell footwear company who created a VR experience on a dangerous mountain trek. 'Trailscape' allowed participants to walk on a specially constructed installation and experience a new level of immersion through hiking on steep slopes in the mountains, passing over a footbridge a few hundred meters above the ground or using ropes and chains.

The use of Artificial Intelligence (AI) was seen by some as a 'game changer' for the creative industry. There have been several good examples of how brands have used AI in producing branded content, but as Ada Lovelace, creator of the first computer algorithm in 1840 said, *"Computers originate nothing; they merely do that which we order them."* Lexus was one of the first brands to use AI technology in scripting a film that about a perplexing story of a self-aware car involved in a televised crash test.

Perhaps the best application for brands using AI is through analytics and a more in-depth understanding of how their content works.

PREFACE

One technique is 'machine learning' - teaching technology to think and operate similarly to humans - to enhance the customer experience. We have seen several examples of how AI has been used effectively, including Toyota Prius, Best Western, McDonald's and Lufthansa.

Brands using audio, predominantly, through Podcasts, has grown exponentially during this period.

There has been a significant increase in devices that are activated through 'voice', including Apple Siri, Amazon Alexa, Google Assistant, Microsoft Cortana and Samsung Bixby. It was Burger King's 'Google Home of the Whopper' stunt that disrupted the ad-world. It became a catalyst for controversy and conversations around the technology's vulnerability. Apparently, Google was unaware of the content and unamused that it essentially hijacked its software without permission. Other brands that have used audio through Podcasts include, 'The Discovery Adventures' by Landrover Discovery, 'The Message' by GE, 'The Sauce' by McDonald's, #LIPSTORIES by Sephora Collection, 'Open For Business' by eBay and 'Innovation' by Johnson & Johnson.

Gaming and e-Sports has exploded in the past five years. No longer the domain of teenager's spending hours in their rooms on devices, figures from GWI in their report, 'The Gaming Playbook' show that the percentage of gamers aged 55-64 has grown by 32% in two years. It also says that a third of those gaming on handheld devices do so for the story and narrative which works well for brands who are creating entertaining branded content.

As Tim Cook, CEO of Apple said, *"Gaming has kind of evolved a bit. More people play on portable devices..."*. It's no surprise that this growth in gaming is inextricably linked to the continuous improvement in smart devices. There has also been an increase in betting companies becoming involved, particularly, with e-Sports competitions. An excellent example of this being Unibet, with the first e-Sports and betting collaboration on Snapchat. They followed one of the best Counter Strike: Global Offensive teams in the world called Astralis, with there be #TheSixthMan campaign.

The way that brands reach their audiences has fundamentally changed, primarily with the growing power of social media platforms, such as Instagram and Tik Tok. The disrupters in the broadcasting industry, Netflix and [Amazon] Prime Video has meant that brands have needed to be a great deal smarter when deciding their distribution strategy.

PREFACE

As Bernard Arnault, Chairman & Chief Executive of luxury group LVMH, said, *"If you control your distribution, you control your image."* It has been something that has often been overlooked and left to the 'last minute', but as we move forward to a world of a highly 'distracted' consumers, it will become even more important to get this right from the beginning of the strategic process.

To continue the theme of disruption, we have seen a growing number of brands that have disrupted the 'status quo'. This was apparent when the likes of Uber and Air BnB became multi-billion-dollar businesses. These brands don't own anything particularly tangible, in the case of Uber, their greatest assets are their drivers and for Air BnB, their hosts.

Another fascinating example are Dollar Shave Club, founded by entrepreneur, Michael Dubin, who have taken on the huge multinationals Gillette and Wilkinson's to offer a more reasonably priced shaving kit. They have used branded to great effect to build a successful multi-million-dollar business. According to Sir Richard Branson, *"an entrepreneur is an innovator, a job creator, a game-changer, a business leader, a disruptor, an adventurer."*

A growing trend has been brand activism and purpose-driven marketing. We have seen how this has come to the fore, since the 'Black Lives Matter' movement and how consumers have increasingly expected brands to speak out about important social issues. Other examples include Nike's 'Just Don't Do It' campaign, Bodyform's 'Womb Stories' and Brewdog's Forest, where they will plant one million trees becoming the first carbon-negative global beer business.

One of the most active in the area of sustainability is outdoor clothing brand, Patagonia, that has put this purpose at the heart of their business and content marketing. Yvon Chouniard, founder and CEO, says, *"to do good, you actually have to do something."* Their 'Artifishal' feature-length film is about people, rivers, and the fight for the future of wild fish and the environment that supports them. It explores wild salmon's slide toward extinction, threats posed by fish hatcheries and fish farms, and our continued loss of faith in nature.

The most fundamental incident that occurred during this period was the global pandemic. This has had a huge impact on all areas of our lives and also the world of communications, marketing, production and content creation. There were sweeping proclamations about 'the end of commuting', 'the demise of retail' and 'drastic reduction in air travel'.

PREFACE

Many brands realised that brand messaging at this time of crisis, felt like a tightrope for most, bringing a huge challenge of striking the right tone whilst putting out compelling content.

Any brand message that could be seen to be exploiting the situation would be met with negative consumer sentiment that could cause long term damage to brand equity.

At the same time, many of the traditional ways of creating marketing content, such as production, was severely restricted during lockdown period. Several notable brands pivoted to practically help – Pernod and BrewDog manufactured hand sanitiser to Burberry donating Personal Protective Equipment (PPE) to the UK's National Health Service (NHS). These initiatives have rightly been applauded.

We are now in a world of 'influence' and where brands must entertain to sell more of their products or services. That is why branded content remains the dominant marketing discipline of the 21st century and will continue to grow exponentially.

– A.C.

FOREWORD
Sir John Hegarty

In the early 1960's Andy Warhol painted a picture of a soup can, immortalising the Campbell's name forever, creating an icon that has captured the world's imagination. Even earlier, Titian the great 16th century Venetian artist in his painting 'The Annunciation', placed a clear glass decanter in the bottom right corner of the canvas.

Was this the earliest example of product placement or even branded content?

Of course, many art historians would refute this claim, but they would accept that Venetian artists were prone to not only paint some of the finest pictures ever seen but also were happy to feature within them the superiority of their fellow Venetian craftsmen. Which is why that glass decanter appears in 'The Annunciation'.

Whatever we think of these two examples what it does prove is that we've always been fascinated in communicating our commercial expertise in ways and in places that captured our audience's imagination. Employing creativity to highlight our message.

The explosion of digital media has enabled that craft to expand exponentially. Content has become the new place to go. But within that explosion of opportunity lays also its vulnerability. Irrelevance.

The Branded Content Marketing Association's (BCMA) aim is to counter this with their experience, their awards and highlighting their 3 pillars of excellence, educate, entertain, and inform. Within these 3 pillars lie the secret to successful branded content. You could in fact argue any content.

At the foundation of any piece of communication, lays the simple principle of effectiveness.

Like any piece of work, if it doesn't get noticed, it doesn't work.

Just because you can communicate it doesn't mean you should. Too much of what we create is irrelevant and time wasting. A cardinal sin as far as I'm concerned. We are all of us 'time poor'.

FOREWORD

Creating work of value is our core responsibility, making sure it's noticed is essential. I have the feeling that too much of what we produce becomes 'digital landfill'. The delete button is one of technology's greatest advances. Our aim should be to make it irrelevant.

This is the mission the BCMA are on, their obsession with effectiveness is well founded and their 3 pillars a guide to ensuring that is achieved.

Looking back, I think we can take some guidance from Titian and Warhol, who certainly challenged our perception of what creativity is and what it could achieve. They would, I'm sure, have said why should anyone bother looking at this? And added another pillar, be daring.

John.

Sir John Hegarty is the Founder, Creative of Bartle Bogle Hegarty (BBH) and Co-founder of The Garage Soho. John Hegarty has been central to the global advertising scene over six decades working with brands such as Levi's, Audi, Boddingtons, Lynx, British Airways and Johnnie Walker. He was a founding partner of Saatchi and Saatchi in 1970. He founded Bartle Bogle Hegarty in 1982 with John Bartle and Nigel Bogle. The Agency now has offices in London, New York, Singapore, Stockholm, Shanghai, Mumbai and Los Angeles. John's creative awards are numerous. He has been given the D&AD President's Award for outstanding achievement and in 2014 was admitted to the US AAF Hall of Fame. John was awarded a Knighthood by the Queen in 2007 and was the recipient of the first Lion of St Mark award at the Cannes Festival of Creativity in 2011. John wrote his first book 'Hegarty on Advertising – Turning Intelligence into Magic' in 2011 and his book "Hegarty on Creativity - there are no rules" was published in 2014. In 2014 John Co-founded The Garage Soho, an early-stage investor company that believes in building brands, not just businesses.

PROFESSOR JONATHAN HARDY
Rules And Guidance Needed To Grow Responsible Branded Content Marketing

The contribution I'd like to make is to explore, with the BCMA, the wider industry and stakeholders, what kinds of rules and guidance are needed to grow responsible branded content marketing. So, I'm delighted to be leading a three-year international research initiative, the Branded Content Governance Project, that will explore, share and discuss these findings.

Researchers at the University of the Arts London (UAL), where I am based, the University of Stirling and Complutense University, Madrid are working alongside an international network of academic and industry advisers to create a map of branded-content practices and regulation that seeks to inform policymaking and aid wider public understanding and debate. It will also provide insights and recommendations for managing and regulating communications in the digital age.

From September 2022, the project, jointly funded by the UK Economic and Social and Arts and Humanities Research Councils (ESRC and AHRC), will provide a detailed, cross-national mapping of the emerging rules and practices for branded content across Europe, the US, Canada, and Australia. The second stage of analysis will involve UK and Spanish research teams, who will investigate in greater detail how branded content governance is practised and understood by practitioners, policy actors and stakeholders, and discussed within professional and public media.

Branded content takes many different forms, giving rise to different kinds of problems that need to be carefully delineated. That's an argument I develop in my book, Branded Content: the fateful merging of media and marketing (Routledge, 2021). Most brands' owned media is readily identified as speaking on behalf of the brand, but greater problems arise when marketing communications merge with ostensibly independent media. Here, the expansion of native advertising and sponsored editorial content that occurred in the BCMA's first fifteen years, has been joined by the rapid growth of influencer marketing over the last five years. Worldwide, influencer marketing grew at twice the rate of advertising overall in 2017, with double-digit growth forecast from 2021.

PROFESSOR JONATHAN HARDY
Rules And Guidance Needed To Grow Responsible Branded Content Marketing

We want to identify and examine how industry practitioners and trade bodies, regulators and stakeholders are managing and evaluating the process of creating and enforcing rules for such fast-evolving practices.

Starting from a more aerial view, some of the key issues can be located within two paradoxes. The first is that since 1966 the leading international code of advertising (first created in 1937 by the International Chamber of Commerce) has clear rules on the identification of advertisements. This requires that 'advertisements should be clearly distinguishable as such, whatever their form and whatever the medium used' (ICC 1966: 8; ICC 2018). That 1966 wording is instructive, because it is not anachronistic; it has the scope to include influencer marketing today, or indeed any of the new and hybrid digital ad-formats that began to emerge from the 1990s, three decades after it was written. Yet, we have witnessed waves of integrated and disguised ads in the digital era. The second paradox sits within the first. There has been increasing regulatory, and self-regulatory, action and guidance worldwide in the period since the US Federal Trade Commission (2015) produced updated guidance on native advertising, yet also mounting non-observance. In the UK, we have seen action by the Competition and Markets Authority and the Advertising Standards Authority, comprising code guidance, rulings, monitoring, warnings and friendly advice such as the ASA's (2021b) infographic for ITV's Love Island participants. Yet, when the ASA (2021a: 3) conducted follow-up research on Instagram influencers, published in March 2021, it found, in something of an understatement, 'a disappointing overall rate of compliance with the rules on making it sufficiently clear when they were being paid to promote a product or service'. In fact, 65 per cent of the content it deemed to be marketing communications was not compliant. Similarly, Australia's self-regulator Ad Standards (2021) found widespread breaches of the distinguishable advertising rules amid rising consumer complaints about influencer marketing on social media.

So, what can and should be done? I hope one way in which an academic lens can contribute is in underscoring, and supporting, the argument that the governance of complex, adaptive systems like digital marketing and communications, needs to be multi-level, connective and responsive. There is no single source for effective governance, instead everything that generates and influences 'rules', from the informal discussions between practitioners, to guidance like the BCMA's Influencer Marketing Best Practice Guidelines (BCMA 2021), through to the more formal measures of self-regulatory organisations, like the ASA, and statutory law and regulation, needs to be activated.

PROFESSOR JONATHAN HARDY
Rules And Guidance Needed To Grow Responsible Branded Content Marketing

And there is another profound shift from the old world, the increasing role of automation in rulemaking and governance, from Instagram incentivising those using ad-labelling by granting access to richer data, to the ASA and other self-regulatory organisations increasing their large-scale data monitoring capabilities.

There is a strong argument that the best regulation comes when marketing practitioners support effective self-regulation. While I agree this should always feature, it is coming under strain on many fronts as the legacy of divergent treatment of the press, broadcasting and online creates increasing anomalies across converging communications. Self-regulation is also becoming increasingly challenging for influencer marketing. First, there are powerful drivers to disguise marketing to bypass consumer barriers to engagement. Second, influencers' cultivation of authenticity can be in tension with the acknowledgement of paid promotion. Third, many of the mostly under-35 creators on Instagram and TikTok, and the nano-influencers on all platforms, are outside the professional relationships and support structures that dominated public communications in the pre-digital era. To highlight one anomaly, in the UK self-publishing social media content creators have stronger obligations to disclose gifts, brand payment or other economic considerations than newspaper editors or professional journalists do, yet usually lack access to the in-house legal advice available to the latter. While we have seen a rapid growth of self-service platforms and talent agencies, there are key challenges to address the training needs, support and welfare of all those influencers and emerging content creators along this expanded professional-amateur spectrum, as well as their viewers and readers. For these reasons, I believe we do need to discuss updating legislation to underpin better governance, but this goes even further. If the identification of advertising still matters, then we need to revive a discussion that some may feel is over and done with. Namely, a discussion about separating advertising and media, and so what a suitably 21st century version of separation might comprise.

Note:

The Branded Content Governance Project (2022-2025) is part of the work of the University of the Arts London's Branded Content Research Hub (BCRH). The Hub explores content that is funded or produced by marketers and investigates branded content practices and regulations. You can find out more about the work of BCRH by using this link[1].

---

1 https://www.arts.ac.uk/colleges/london-college-of-communication/research-at-lcc/branded-content-research-hub

PROFESSOR JONATHAN HARDY
Rules And Guidance Needed To Grow Responsible Branded Content Marketing

Jonathan Hardy is Professor of Communications and Media at the London College of Communication, part of the University of the Arts London. He is Principal Investigator for the Branded Content Governance Project. He writes and comments on media industries, media and advertising, communications regulation, and international media systems. His books include Branded Content: the Fateful Merging of Media and Marketing (2021), Critical Political Economy of the Media (2014), Cross-Media Promotion (2010), and Western Media Systems (2008). He is co-editor of The Advertising Handbook (2009/2018) and is series editor of Routledge Critical Advertising Studies. He is a member of the editorial boards of Digital Journalism, Political Economy of Communication, Mediterranean Journal of Communication, and TripleC: Communication, Capitalism & Critique.

References:

Ad Standards (2021) 'Updates to AiMCO's Influencer Marketing Code of Practice', 25 August. https://adstandards.com.au/article/updates-aimco%E2%80%99s-influencer-marketing-code-practice

Advertising Standards Authority (2021a) Influencer monitoring report, 18 March, London: ASA. https://www.asa.org.uk/resource/influencer-monitoring-report-march-2021.html

Advertising Standards Authority (2021b) 'ABC Cheatsheet for Love Island contestants, celebs and influencers', 5 August, London: ASA. https://www.asa.org.uk/resource/abc-cheatsheet-for-love-island.html

BCMA (2021) BCMA Influencer Marketing Best Practice Guidelines, London: BCMA. https://www.thebcma.info/landing-pages/bcma-influencer-marketing-guidelines.html

Federal Trade Commission (2015) Commission Enforcement Policy Statement on Deceptively Formatted Advertisements, 22 December, Washington: FTC. https://www.ftc.gov/legallibrary/browse/commission-enforcement-policy-statement-deceptively-formatted-advertisements

Hardy, J. (2021) Branded Content: The Fateful Merging of Media and Marketing, Abingdon, Oxon: Routledge. https://routledge.pub/branded-content

International Chamber of Commerce (1966) International Code of Advertising Practice, Paris: ICC.

International Chamber of Commerce (2018) ICC Advertising and Marketing Communications Code, Paris: ICC. https://iccwbo.org/publication/icc-advertising-and-marketing-communications-code/

DR. HELEN POWELL
Are We There Yet? The Temporal Dynamics Of Motoring Branded Content

> *"You cannot bore people into buying your product, you can only interest them in buying it."*
> **David Ogilvy**

The petrol price hike in July 2022 saw motorists paying more than ever at the pumps. Brought about by a series of factors including the war in Ukraine and a fall in the value of the pound against the dollar fuel reached a record high with diesel creeping over £2 per litre. Why this did not prompt a falling out of love with motoring, or at least a significant cutting back in driving activity is interesting and the subject of investigation here. Indeed, from the earliest days of the car, it has always been about more than engineering, performance and speed. Pioneered by the introduction of the Michelin Guide (1900) branded content remains a successful tool for car promotion as it effectively and affectively brings to life the joy of motoring, a leisure activity centred around a journey that fuses both a temporal and physical dimension.

Promotional strategies have always been about space and time: where to position the ad and how long it will run. Where branded content differs is that it does not use these as the framework around which content is built but rather time and space become vessels for the possible in terms of creativity. More specifically, how branded content treats time differently to traditional advertising centres on the concept of duration: time as a qualitative value to be filled with experiences allowing people to spend time with the brand.

When we travel it is highly experiential. We are mobile, in transit, and that which connects departure to arrival is the time it takes to get there. The journey can therefore be harnessed as a liminal space for brand relationship building.

At the beginning of the twentieth century perceptions of the car were changing within both the motoring world and indeed in the public consciousness. Whilst recognised as a significant luxury item, print car advertising at this time principally centred on two dimensions: its aspirational qualities and its technical merits, all communicated in a static 2D format on the page.

DR. HELEN POWELL
Are We There Yet?
The Temporal Dynamics Of Motoring Branded Content

The Michelin Guide (1900) challenged the advertising establishment via a model whereby, whilst still utilising print, brands would be the generators of their own content to build a more effective and authentic relationship with their target audience. In this respect, what the Michelin Guide sought to achieve was ahead of its time by over a century. In today's social media era brands struggle to function as custodians of their own identity.

However, the Michelin brothers, André and Édouard, devised the guide to generate interest in motoring and inherently the tyres they were manufacturing but more than this their legacy lies in the way that they utilised promotional content to control their brand identity through ownership of the concept of motoring. Indeed, their own strategy for growth centred on increasing annual car mileage and hence the need for new tyres as part of regular maintenance – Michelin tyres of course. Focusing on 'the journey' rather than a specific car in order to engineer broader appeal, the early editions included maps to reach identified beauty spots, locations of petrol pumps, and technical instructions around car maintenance. It was only later, following World War One, that the guide evolved into what we know now whereby a quintessential part of its increasing popularity came from its inclusion of a star rating of restaurants mapped along a route and awarded by hired professional food critics. Initially distributed for free, as the guide became valued by motorists so did it then come with a price attached. The Guide is now sold in 93 countries.

In essence, what we have is a travel, hotel and restaurant guide for French motorists produced by a tyre company and as such is an early example of the power of branded content to feed off the capacity of popular culture but re-packaged to offer both relevancy and entertainment value and delivered by a more discrete brand custodian. As a pioneer in the field, the value of the Michelin Guide is in how it saw the journey as opposed to car ownership and tyre consumption as worthy of promotion. Rather than working with the duality of the car and its driver the publication offers up a more dialogic relationship: man, and machine crafting motoring adventures together. As a result, at the heart of the Michelin Guide was a cultivation of the pleasure of driving and the emotions attached to it. Today journeys may be regulated by work, namely commuting, or as antidote, an escape from the quotidian. What links such activities and offers up a unique promotional space as a result is that within the car we are imbibed with a sense of temporal freedom: seemingly de-synchronised from those around us and yet operating in a context of always being on hyper sensory alert.

DR. HELEN POWELL
Are We There Yet?
The Temporal Dynamics Of Motoring Branded Content

Temporality can be distinguished from clock time through the injection of the lived experience, turning the linear progression of quantitative minutes and seconds into a deeper qualitative immersive vessel. Branded content is ripe here to fill such temporal moments in relation to motoring promotion through a recognition that the temporal space a journey carves out allows us to spend time with a brand in a non-distracting manner. When so much of the diurnal centres on clock-watching, the car as cocoon crafts its own temporal register specific only to that one journey. In the car, our attention is focused, separated from the usual array of distraction of the multi-screen landscape. In the development of promotional culture, branded content comes out of consumers turning their backs on the push model of advertising. They recognise that time is precious and the amount of content available is gargantuan and they want to choose what they see and hear and when. The content itself to be effective needs to be reflective of brand personality but laced with currency; carefully curated to achieve its goals.

The legacy of the Michelin Guide in the annals of the history of branded content is both significant and enduring. Over a century later Land Rover was an early adopter of the now ubiquitous podcast medium. Storytelling is an inherent part of the human condition. Stories shape who we are and can make us feel the whole gamut of emotions. They shape our daily lives at the macro and micro level and at the same time have the ability to take us out of this world in terms of both space and time.

Land Rover podcasts speak to the recognition that whilst the car is in motion, there is actually little movement from the driver, but in contrast all senses are heightened. Working with Mindshare in 2017 and utilising the in-car immersive experience of 3D sound, the Discovery Adventures were aimed at existing Land Rover owners and aspirant consumers. This seven-part mystery series starts in London's Natural History Museum where a child named Sam, his uncle and his Dog, Rover, of course, seek to solve the mystery of national GPS disruptions. As they travel through the country the listener takes the part of Sam and picks up clues provided by various celebrities that populate the story.

Narrated by renowned outdoor experts, families work together as a captive audience in this adventure. And yet ultimately it is the car that is the star as it propels us forward into the narrative. It is interesting that time was a key driver in the forging of the overall idea.

DR. HELEN POWELL
Are We There Yet?
The Temporal Dynamics Of Motoring Branded Content

As Scott Dicken, the Marketing Director of Jaguar Land Rover UK stated on launch:

> *"The car is a unique environment, a place of reduced distractions that allows for important quality time, and we're hoping to encourage families and adventurers of all ages to make the most of this time together to go on a car adventure."*

On the back of its success Land Rover Stories (2020) is a series of video-driven, Instagram-promoted travelogues in which photographers document their adventures driving their Land Rovers across a global landscape. This is then developed in a second phase where famous partners such as John Mayer share their journeys too. In this beautiful fusion of image and narrative the journey once again is both centred and captured but in such a way as to spark interest for the self-creation of future plans.

Authenticity is key for successful branded content. Branded content is all about storytelling: how the brand tells stories about itself in different ways. Both the Michelin brothers and Land Rover successfully executed their mission by playing with the dual and yet interwoven nature of the concept of journey.

The car allows the journey to exist but when journeys become adventures, the promotional possibilities are endless.

Dr. Helen Powell PFHEA, is Associate Professor, Creative Advertising and Course Director, Creative Advertising with Marketing. Helen is also the Interim Director of Education and Student Experience, School of Arts and Creative Industries at London South Bank University.

MAYA BOGLE
Can purpose-led brands deliver better results?

The path to purchase is more complex than ever with consumers expecting more from brands. Traditional forms of tactical, and activation marketing, may simply not work hard enough to build up brand affinity, desirability, and that elusive path to purchase.

Both our personal instincts, and evidence, shows that consumers are more likely to buy from companies they recognise as standing for something over and above their profitability. Today, more than ever, a brand's values are evidently as important as their products with 64%[1] of consumers preferring to buy from companies with a purpose-driven reputation. Consumers are engaging with brands they can trust, respect and who they believe are genuinely trying to make a difference rather than just extolling their virtues.

Ben & Jerry's brought integrity and activism to an ice-cream brand. Dove is boosting self-esteem around the world. Patagonia is committed to environmentalism and Tesla's mission to change the world through a transition to sustainable energy goes beyond the auto industry.

Business leaders are challenged with making their purpose clear and sharing their values throughout their entire business model - including their creative. And no, that doesn't just mean slapping a rainbow on a logo during LGBTQ+ pride month - it could include how they source their creative work too.

A possible route to achieving this would be to consider open sourcing as an alternative. At its heart, open sourcing has the ambition to open doors to all creatives. Democratising access to the creative industries is a huge ambition, but if one believes that a great idea can come from anywhere, a platform-based approach must surely stack up.

A true meritocracy would allow the creative's work to shine through and not be influenced by the colour of their skin, their sexuality, faith, economic background, education, or location.

---

[1] https://www.havasgroup.com/press_release/havas-meaningful-brands-report-2021-finds-we-are-entering-the-age-of-cynicism/

MAYA BOGLE
Can purpose-led brands deliver better results?

The open-sourcing model gives creatives from all backgrounds, disciplines and experiences the power of having their work seen by the right people in the right places and to get discovered. This would help break down the many barriers that creatives face, including the age-old challenge of 'you need experience to get a job, but you need a job to get experience'.

Open sourcing delivers creative content that truly resonates with audiences as it is often made by creatives who are a subset of the actual target market. What better way to demonstrate a commitment to inclusivity, than by working with a truly diverse group of authentic creators from every walk of life, from every location, colour, faith, sexuality, socioeconomic, and educational background? To be known as a brand that has made a positive social and economic impact on the global creative community.

If a brand is going to 'talk the talk', it's important to 'walk the walk' and they can help democratise the creative process by adopting a different way of sourcing their creative content. By doing so, they'll engage creatives who intrinsically can immerse a brand into popular culture, delivering a process that creates a dialogue with your consumers rather than the dated monologue that dictated so much of historical marketing.

A brand will achieve multiple pieces of beautiful, fresh, original work and stories to flood their channels rather than just one hero piece of work – as well as a valuable connection with the creative community.

By engaging the global community of creatives for localised, diverse, authentic creative work a brand can be positioned as a hero that champions creativity. It's not even necessary to engage creatives for actual branded content – think of the power of a brand being attached to thousands of pieces of work by sponsoring creatives to produce work around climate change, black rights, gay rights, and more, whilst simultaneously creating an opportunity for exposure, recognition and income for the creative that made the work. A beautiful model that supports both the brand, the creative and a higher purpose.

Ultimately creativity is important in every industry. Creativity inspires people. It can serve to inform, unite, to challenge attitudes and prejudice and to mobilise wider communities into taking positive action.

MAYA BOGLE
Can purpose-led brands deliver better results?

Creativity has the power to stop people in their tracks and change the way they think about black rights, gay rights, women's rights, poverty, climate change or any of the Sustainable Development Goals. Creativity has both power and impact. At its best, creativity can change the world and make it a better place - not just a more beautiful place.

Brands have got the opportunity to do so much good and there are clearly demonstrable benefits in adopting this philosophy...

Do good and do better as a brand.

Maya Bogle is the Co-Founder of Talenthouse, the largest co-creation platform in the world. Maya is driven by the Talenthouse mission to support and nurture creatives at every stage of their career, by giving them access to opportunities for recognition, inspiration, learning, collaboration, and income. She is passionate about democratising access to the creative industries and believes that a great idea can come from anywhere. She's never lost sight of the importance of craft - that it is ultimately great creative work that sits at the heart of great marketing - yet she embraces the many changes that the industry has gone through and the importance of digital in shaping how work is delivered. She is championing the ad industry to embrace the Talenthouse model as an effective way to engage creatives for high quality, diverse, localised, and culturally relevant creative work and impact across multiple markets and channels. Maya is a regular speaker at global industry conferences including Cannes Lions, Social Media Week, Advertising Week, Media Summit, Web Summit, f.ounders, NOAH, ISBA, The Marketing Society, Soho House, the Content Marketing Association and many more. Maya also enjoys coaching and mentoring and speaks at numerous educational establishments as well as judging creative awards throughout the industry. Maya is a member of the BCMA UK Advisory Board.

GORDON GLENISTER
The Rise And Rise Of Influencer Marketing

There isn't anyone that doesn't know what the word influencer means. The world of influencer marketing has taken over our lives with more and more of us trusting the opinions of others than traditional advertising. As consumers a lot of us 'hate' ads, we ignore them, we block them, we avoid banner and search ads.

The industry is expected to be on course for $16bn in 2022/3 and now 80-90% of brands are either investing in the media or considering it.

So, what is an influencer? An influencer is someone who can change the behaviour of others through knowledge, trusted opinion, and content creation. Therefore, influencer marketing is the ability to promote a product or service through an individual (influencer).

However, not everyone will refer to themselves as an influencer yet still have an engaged audience and has the ability to 'influence'. They are often referred to as a digital creator, content creator, entrepreneur, author, speaker, journalist, travel blogger, foodie, vlogger, fitness coach, gamer, celebrity, academic, sports star, community group leader, model and so on.

Why do we follow content creators?

It's important in executing a campaign to understand our motivators in why we follow content creators. According to a survey completed by Influencer.com and Global Web Index (see over), learning something new still tops the list. Social media has allowed us to explore new content at scale in a way traditional media couldn't do. How many people say I have been on Clubhouse or TikTok for hours? Scrolling through content is a way to pass the time, which means that content must be uplifting, inspirational or entertaining to a whole new level for it to stand out.

During the Global Pandemic the Body Coach Joe Wicks had the whole nation captivated with his workout sessions. Many of us discovered content creators particularly fitness ones for the first time and have remained loyal to them ever since.

GORDON GLENISTER
The Rise And Rise Of Influencer Marketing

MAIN MOTIVATORS TO FOLLOW CONTENT CREATORS
% of consumers who follow influencers that cite these reasons for following content creators

51% To learn something new

49% For entertaining/uplifting content

49% To pass the time

43% Shared interests /passions

38% To gain inspiration

37% News updates

30% To learn about new brands/products

27% To feel motivated/challenged

23% To keep up with professional news

23% To do an activity (e.g. follow a workout)

22% To see their lifestyles /see things I can't see in real life

14% To get access to promo codes /discounts

globalwebindex.com | influencer.com

Gen-Z and Millennials are increasingly discovering their news and finding out about new products through their favourite content creators (influencers). Conscious mainstream news outlets were missing out in 2022, BBC and Sky News started to highlight news snippets about the war in Ukraine on TikTok which have received high levels of engagement. Content creators offer expertise in just about every discipline, so those that are really good at what they do are totally focused on their 'niche' and consistent with their posting.

What can Influencers do for brands?

Consumers trust the opinions of their favourite content creators because they are knowledgeable about their subject and can talk about it with authority. Working with an influencer that matches your brand values and target audience can be a great way to build trust in a brand. Influencers have engaged audiences which brands want to tap into. Working with an influencer on a campaign can help tell a brand story in an authentic and genuine way sometimes even far better than the brands own advertising message.

GORDON GLENISTER
The Rise And Rise Of Influencer Marketing

In turn by having a mix of influencers with varying demographics, can help build brand awareness in new markets and drive conversions and in terms of cost, you can engage with an influencer for a few hundred dollars for a post or video. Of course, it depends on the scale of their audience, but it can be an extremely cost-effective way to promote a brand through influencers. Let's also not forget that the comments and engagement provide real-time feedback on a brand message unlike almost any other form of media channel. Blogs and videos can remain published for months, years post campaign, even in some instances, in perpetuity so that the earned media return can be considerable.

Sponsored posts, stories or videos

This is one of the most popular ways to engage an influencer by paying them for a one-off post or a series of posts and stories ensuring the brand is tagged and clearly. These posts can be used to support a new product launch or just part of an ongoing brand campaign.

Ambassador programs

The best performing campaigns are those involving influencers in ambassador programs, because they are invested a lot more in the brand and their audiences are used to seeing that brand associated with their favourite influencer on a regular basis.

Competitions and challenges

Some of the best campaigns are ones involving challenges or competitions because it's fun exciting and can have a viral impact.

Guest blogging

This is when an influencer is writing a blog on your website or on their website about your products.

Social media takeover

Influencers are social media experts, and so it's a consideration to employ them to run the campaign for you as well.

GORDON GLENISTER
The Rise And Rise Of Influencer Marketing

Research/white papers

Influencers have knowledge in their chosen niches, so many brands will co-create content with them. The Talkwalker annual social media trends report[1] engages several thought leaders to add their tips on what the future looks like, adds their profile too and of course what do we all do but share it on social. This is more common with B2B influencers.

Livestream education/demos/selling

This is exploded over the last year having been huge in Asia. Influencers are not merely brand ambassadors but through their trust and knowledge many can sell and demo products at scale. Aware of this demand Alibaba and Amazon in 2020 advertised for 100, 000 influencers for their platforms. Brands are using affiliate marketing methods to drive conversions.

Inviting influencers to attend events

Influencers love exclusive access to events because they want exclusive content for their audiences. Inviting them to speak be part of a panel or turn up to take content can be a highly effective way to create social buzz.

Podcast collaborations

Content creators can be guests on your podcasts, or you can sponsor their own one. I host the Influence Global Podcast[2] in partnership with the BCMA that shines a spotlight on the influencer marketing industry, and we have had some amazing influencers on our podcast.

What to look for in an influencer

Finding the right influencers remains the biggest challenge for brands which is why there are over 1,300 influencer platforms aiming to service this need. Agencies add another dimension in that they do the whole lot for the brand, because don't underestimate how much communication is involved in running an influencer campaign at scale.

1 https://www.talkwalker.com/social-media-trends
2 https://podcasts.apple.com/gb/podcast/influence-global-podcast-shining-a-spotlight-on/id1463375054

GORDON GLENISTER
The Rise And Rise Of Influencer Marketing

Influencers reject at least 70% of direct messages and emails so getting them to respond is an artform within itself. So, what do you need to look for when considering an influencer: -

Brand affinity: is the influencer content/and follower interest linked to the relevant brand. If you were working for a spice brand and wanted to find food influencers, is their content all food related?

Engagement: one of the single most important requirements is how responsive the influencer is to their audience and vice versa by comments and likes. Instagram average engagement is around 1.7%. You are likely to get a higher engagement level from a micro or nano influencer.

Demographic split: if the brand is female targeted, you would want an influencer with a high percentage of their followers being female. This applies to age split too. If the brand wants a younger audience, you will want to see that represented in the influencer's follower base.

Geo-location: if the brand was UK based and only sold in the UK you would want to see a high percentage of their followers residing in the UK otherwise its wasted media.

Audience quality: how much of their audience is genuine, i.e., not bought or Bots. The most important aspect of choosing an influencer is to have a deep understand of the quality and relevance of their audience. Many of the influencer platforms have access to this information. A manual search will not establish this.

Competitor posts: have they been promoting your competitors.

Profanity: check video content too. Some of the biggest youtubers have used explicit language which is a safety concern for some brands.

Organic v Sponsored: you don't want to engage with a market trading influencer who is promoting every other product – this will not create great engagement and not support follower growth.

Content quality: are the photos, and video editing of a high standard – the competition now is so high that audiences won't stand for poor quality audio, graphics or transitions.

GORDON GLENISTER
The Rise And Rise Of Influencer Marketing

Consistent posting: how regular is the creator posting – you would want to see daily or at the very worst 3 times a week.

Finally, I would add that the most important consideration in influencer marketing is to constantly evaluate and optimise. The sector is here to stay and those that are at the top of the game are generating significant returns, in some instances, as much as 11x greater Return On Investment (ROI) versus other media when done well.

Gordon Glenister is the Global Head Of Influencer Marketing at the Branded Content Marketing Association, Chief Strategy Officer of global influencer agency Audience2Media, Author of best selling book Influencer Marketing Strategy, host of Influence Global Podcast and online columnist for the London Evening Standard.

SIMON ORPIN
Drive To Thrive

Brand integration (good old product placement) in content continues to develop, especially via sponsorship in the UK. The recent M&S tie up with *Cooking with the Stars* included a huge number of branded VO's during the show that took prominence to a level almost of the ilk of Coles in the Australian version of *MasterChef*.

At Electric Glue we recently integrated live property data from our Rightmove client as an interstitial linking their property data to the specific region being reviewed on the Channel 4 property show *Location, Location, Location*. We also integrated our coffee client, Caffe Latte, into the current series of *Love Island* as the official coffee partner (the contestants love an iced coffee). This extended to licencing opportunities in store to huge amounts of bespoke content shot on set and distributed socially, including developing a 'money can't buy' competition mechanic.

However, how much more compelling is it when the content itself is supporting a brand proposition in a credible and meaningful manner?

There are many examples of this content creation strategy but I have a particular favourite.

Drive to Survive.

Produced via Box to Box, production was led by James Gay-Rees. This was a key aspect of the project, using a producer with a great reputation for filming similar style content (he was the person behind the famous Senna documentary in 2010) and therefore, the expertise to create relevant and engaging content.

The idea was initially planned as a Red Bull specific project (a company with an exemplary record in ground-breaking content creation after all) but widened to a Formula 1™ initiative was seen to be an ideal route for the ambitions of Liberty Media who have owned F1 since 2017. At the time, their objective was to build on F1's profile since the Eccleston era, especially in the US, which was seen as a primary territory for growth.

SIMON ORPIN
Drive To Thrive

The positioning of the Netflix series as a humanisation of the sport introduced an emotive, behind the racing helmet, set of personal stories in, around and even away from the track, and appeared to be perfect to deliver on these objectives.

Often in the branded content world, the challenge is measurement, in other words proof that such a strategy can deliver on key business KPI's. So, did the show do that for F1 and for Netflix themselves?

Oh boy did it!

The first series covered the 2018 world championship, premiering on March 8th, 2019. The first challenge was that not every team was keen to be involved, namely Mercedes. However, series 2 followed and episode 4 featured Toto Wolff in a whole show dedicated to the Mercedes team. One can only assume that the exposure of the other teams was proving beneficial (especially in terms of livery sponsorship values) that Toto, himself a 30% owner of Mercedes F1, saw the need to be involved.

Further confirmation of the value of the show to the Formula 1 brand followed in terms of repeat commissions. Series 4 has now aired and has been renewed for a further two years to cover the 2022 and 2023 seasons.

In terms of value to Netflix, *Drive to Survive* is in their top 10 streamed programmes in 56 countries around the world and Number One in 33 of them.

And is appealing to the lucrative, hard to reach 16-34 age group. Of all the new fans attracted to the sport in the last two years, 72% have been in this young demographic and the fan base of the sport is now estimated to be approaching one billion people.

Global audiences have boomed. The current average is a global audience of 70m viewers per race with the most recent Abu Dhabi Grand Prix viewership beating the audience to the Super Bowl (109m simultaneous views versus 101m).

But what about the specific US market that was so important to Liberty Media?

SIMON ORPIN
Drive To Thrive

The first two races of this season saw a 52% increase year on year with the Saudi GP attracting the largest cable audience since 1995.

US revenues via race attendance and merchandising sales are up 60% for the US races. As an indicator, the US races in 2018 attracted 264,000 people to the events over the three days of racing. In 2021, this number had grown to 400,000. And more than half of the self-acclaimed F1 fans accredited *Drive to Survive* as the major influence in their introduction to the sport.

Social Media has also thrived with a 40% growth year on year, approaching some 50m followers around the world.

And the series has also inspired 'spin off' shows such as *Chasing the Dreams* that airs on F1TV focusing on Formula 2, the feeder racing discipline to Formula 1 itself.

Oh, and Liberty Media's share price has risen by 62% since season 1 went to air.

Drive to Thrive indeed.

In fact, with ESPN's TV rights in the US ending next year, there is even speculation that Netflix, despite their well-publicised challenges in the burgeoning SVOD marketplace, will bid to become the next rights holder and play on their recently announced commercial venture with Microsoft Ad Sales. So maybe it will become 'Thrive to Survive'.

All in all, it just goes to show the power of creativity via credible and enjoyable content is a far greater force in marketing than anything else (when done well of course).

Simon Orpin is Co-Founder & CEO of Electric Glue, a pioneering partnership agency backed by the Chairmanship of advertising legend, Sir John Hegarty. They work with content originators to broker innovative partnerships with media owners. Prior to this Simon was Planning Director at ITV where he brought together a successful team that developed a proposition to bring all of ITV's best assets into the world of media planning and creativity. Simon is a member of the BCMA UK Advisory Board.

JEANETTE OKWU
Brand Storytelling Takes Centre-Stage

In a world with no attention span, storytelling takes centre-stage. But telling a story in the digital and post-Corona age is anything but simple. Therefore, I am eternally grateful to organisations like the BCMA for promoting the value of branded content and influencer marketing.

The BCMA is designed for anyone involved in branded content and influencer marketing. So it gives me, in particular, the opportunity to exchange experiences with peers in my industry I would otherwise not have been in contact.

The exchange is extremely valuable as we all tend to 'stew in our own bubble'. Through best practice, the BCMA leads the debate on what makes great branded content and how brands, agencies, platforms, media owners, publishers, and influencers can engage audiences for maximum impact and meaning.

The BCMA invests in research and releasing best practice guides that are valuable to mastering the day-to-day intricacies of influencer marketing. One of its unique features is its Resource Hub, which is full of helpful information from articles, webinars, and papers.

Polls and events always guarantee a lively and engaged audience. Members are just a click away if I want to network or have a question that needs answering.

Learning is at the core of the BCMA, and as any marketer knows today, learning is the one thing we can not do our job without.

Therefore, I am excited to participate in creating material that allows for experiential learning in an ever-changing influencer marketing landscape.

This way, we can create the opportunity to connect with the leading experts in the branded content and influencer marketing industries.

JEANETTE OKWU
Brand Storytelling Takes Centre-Stage

Some topics that are top of mind in influencer marketing are:

- **With word-of-mouth through social media driving purchasing decisions, influencer marketing is unlikely to disappear, but how do brands need to adjust their strategies.**
- **How influencers have mastered working from home - what we learn from them to improve our experiences and what not to do.**
- **The influencer ecosystem may be shifting, but there are ways brands can adapt to the 'new normal' and continue to build brand equity.**
- **Tactics for brands that focus on community building over selling products and non-contrived partnerships.**
- **It's a marathon, not a sprint.**

One of the biggest challenges in the highly competitive world of influencer marketing is staying afloat with new regulatory changes, new platform features, algorithmic changes, user behaviour, and social developments playing into the advertising and marketing landscape.

The BCMA provides guidance to the industry, ensuring greater consistency around language and behaviours, guiding advertisers and marketers on best practices when engaging in influencer marketing activity.

For me, the organisation is a global 'lightning-rod' as its chapters in many countries operate collectively under an agreed vision with a consistent message, that recognises their local nuances, which is essential when considering hyper-personalisation and bespoke content in campaigns.

Jeanette Okwu is the Founder and CEO of beyondinfluence, an influence & brand ambassador marketing agency helping clients to ride the next wave of marketing. She is a champion and an independent thought leader on social and emerging technologies, with a track record of building and implementing effective integrated marketing and communication initiatives by putting data and storytelling front and center. Jeanette is a member of the BCMA Influence Industry Steering Group.

SIMON BELL

What The Changing Business Models In Streaming Tell Us About The Future Of Branded Content

Part 1: A match made in heaven...by marketers

Growing up I'd often wondered why the likes of *EastEnders*, *Coronation Street* and *Emmerdale* were referred to as 'the Soaps'. It felt like a strange and unusual word for a group of television shows that were such a fixture in our daily lives.

But, like many things, what seems strange on the surface makes a lot of sense when you investigate it.

The origins of the Soap Opera go right back to 1930's America, where radio dramas were created for brand sponsors, who, you guessed it, were selling soap through ads around the radio shows.

From those early days, marketers have always recognised the power of entertainment to attract and engage audiences and built their success through strategies that put the brand alongside entertainment we love - either through advertising or sponsorship.

This relationship, however, has dramatically shifted in the last 20-years...

The emergence of content driven social platforms - firstly YouTube, then Instagram, and now TikTok - means modern marketers have become accustomed to, and experienced in, building their own audiences, and investing in their own forms of content, and branded content has really taken off.

Alongside this, we've seen the meteoric rise of subscription-led streaming platforms, in particular Netflix, which changed our expectations and consumption habits. We have got used to not being interrupted by ads, we've got used to watching what we want when we want it, and we've been living in an era with unprecedented access to high quality content, with Netflix alone spending a staggering $17B on content in 2021.

SIMON BELL
What The Changing Business Models In Streaming Tell Us About The Future Of Branded Content

That's right, $17B a year, which is over $46M every day, or almost $2M every hour. Spent by just one company. With this level of content being paid for, it makes sense why this era is referred to as the 'golden age of content', and it's no exaggeration to say that there's not been investment like this in an artform since 'the Renaissance era in Florence'.

And in the most part, this has been a relatively closed shop, with brand marketers kept out of the equation.

Of course, there are several notable examples, from *Drive to Survive* (F1 and Netflix), *Dads* (Unilever and Apple TV+) and a recent deal struck between Nike and Apple TV+, but up until this point it's been a relatively high bar to entry, with major brands spending significant cash to be able to play in this level of entertainment.

And whilst that might seem like a missed revenue opportunity for streamers, if capital was free flowing and subscribers continued to grow, there was no real imperative to worry about a more extensive brand funded entertainment strategy.

However, that all seems to be changing now.

Part 2: The day it all changed

On Wednesday April 20th, 2022, Netflix share price dropped by more than 30% in one single day, and at time of writing this the price has dropped 70% YTD.

Aside from the macroeconomic conditions all businesses are dealing with in the early 2020s, this has largely been credited to a perceived flatlining/drop in Netflix's growth, with the company reporting a loss of 200K subscribers in Q1 of this year, and warning that potentially that number could increase to 2M by end of the year.

Whether or not the stock price course corrects in time, it's fair to say that this drop sent a shockwave across media and entertainment as the rules seemed to change overnight.

It was no longer ok to invest on the assumption of aggressive future subscriber growth.

SIMON BELL
What The Changing Business Models In Streaming Tell Us About The Future Of Branded Content

For legacy media companies who'd spent years arguing that Netflix had been treated favourably by the markets, only eventually to then invest in their own streaming services, this must leave a bitter taste.

What this means is these businesses now have less cash to play with and need to put more focus on demonstrating revenues. And if you aren't generating more revenue from subscribers, where do you turn to? Advertisers.

We'd already seen the likes of Hulu, Peacock and HBO Max successfully roll out ad supported pricing plans, and now Disney+ and Netflix are set to follow suit, recently announcing a partnership with Microsoft.

Whilst 'ad-supported' could just mean that we are going to be seeing a lot of traditional TV ad spots on our streaming services, I really and truly hope that a company that has built its reputation disrupting what has come before it, doesn't stop when it comes to how it can integrate brand advertising into its product.

This should be a moment where streamers lean into brand funded content and entertainment opportunities in a big way, unlocking for marketers the commercial opportunity that exists in brand funded entertainment, and generating the revenue they need, without disappointing their subscribers and fans - an all-round win-win.

Part 3: The future opportunity for branded content

Whilst the traditional advertising model can't be knocked for its stamina and ability to prevail as a dominant model in brand communications, it's not the best at adapting and innovating, as the old models hold tight.

Creating short ads to place around entertainment might have been pioneering once, but that was almost 100-years ago, and it's time we moved on

As we look to the future, there's more opportunity than ever for a broader variety of brand funded content and entertainment formats. A chance for forward thinking brand marketers, and streamers to get creative about how they can work together to drive the necessary results they both need.

SIMON BELL
What The Changing Business Models In Streaming Tell Us About The Future Of Branded Content

Whilst it's foolish predicting how this will play out, there's two opportunities that I think are worth drawing out:

1. A golden era of original long form brand funded entertainment

We've seen the early leaders in long form brand funded entertainment making moves and investing in the genre, but could we be about to see streamers opening themselves up too many more brand funded entertainment partnerships as they look to expand revenue opportunities?

If the opportunity arises for a broader set of brands to invest in long form entertainment, the ones that make the move first will get the benefit of being able to stand out from their competition, rise above the algorithms driving social media and build relevancy with their audiences.

There's no doubt that long form brand funded entertainment requires commitment, bravery, and investment, but it also offers great value and ROI on that investment, in ways that traditional advertising campaigns seldom do.

With entertainment such a driving force in our culture, there's a clear opportunity to benefit from enormous, earned media, PR, and social conversation - increasing reach and reducing media spend.

Secondly, there's the ability to create a whole campaign ecosystem of assets around the core entertainment itself, and we're not talking about 'cutdowns', or sticking your new TV ad on YouTube here.

If you look at the way broadcasters market their IP, you see that brands can be advertising their content through trailers, experiential, spin off content and more. This kind of joined up experience means brands can truly 'sweat the assets' and make their long form entertainment investment work hard across their marketing ecosystem.

SIMON BELL
What The Changing Business Models In Streaming Tell Us About The Future Of Branded Content

2. A world of opportunity to leverage existing IP

We've outlined the amount of investment that's gone into content in recent years ($17BN being invested in content by Netflix alone in 2021), and as streamers look to generate new revenue streams, how could brands partner with existing entertainment IP in new and innovative ways?

The idea of brand partnerships is not new, and with the recent launch of *Stranger Things* Season 4, we've seen brand partnerships with the likes of Domino's Pizza, MAC Cosmetics, Monopoly and Doritos.

With its cross generational appeal and heady mix of nostalgia and sci-fi, *Stranger Things* is well suited to these types of brand partnerships, but will Netflix start to commission more brand-friendly shows that are designed with brand partnerships in mind?

Alongside this, could brands be given more access to leverage star talent in their own content, or work with showrunners and writers to co-create spin off formats or second screen content that can reach audiences across channels?

There's so much room for growth here, and it feels like a win for both Netflix and brands to be exploring this approach above just selling traditional ad spots around shows.

Only time will tell how this all plays out, but what seems clear to me is that it's a very exciting time to be working in branded content and brand funded entertainment.

Simon Bell is Managing Director at creative content agency, JustSo. Starting out as the studio manager, he was able to draw on his previous work in music radio and broadcast – with BBC 6 Music and XFM – to grow the agency's post-production facilities, while forming strong relationships with clients. In time his job has moved into new-business and includes pitching to potential collaborators and overseeing the early phase of new projects.

SHANNON WALKER
The Evolution Of Creativity To Disrupt Change

The resilience of global content showed the industry's strength in not just being able to survive in a worldwide pandemic but thrive, as content proved it indeed was *king*. At a time when we've never been so isolated, disconnected and separated, brand communication added colour and entertainment to our lives whilst helping us stay connected as active online participants in brand communities.

Creativity has a unique power to unite people, drive change and inspire us to do better

A strong theme of togetherness and increased solidarity against injustice has helped to disrupt positive waves of change to what branded communication looks like. Consequently, we have entered arguably one of the most creatively diverse times the industry has seen: as marketers challenged unconscious biases, teams diversified their talent and knowledge gaps were filled around empathetic marketing, cultural intelligence, and the power that representation plays in shaping how we view each other.

From fashion brands platforming inspiring personalities with disabilities to front campaigns to amplification of poly-cultural individuals and families flickered on TV screens - the mounting pressure to represent a rich plethora of people both in front of the camera and behind the scenes has become a core priority for most marketers and brands wanting to do better. Whilst strides are still to be made on the topics of diversity, equality and pay gaps, the more this is normalised in content, the more we will see it actualised in real life.

At the heart of this change has been the evolving values-driven consumer, who is hyper-aware that 'you are what you consume'. For this mindful and savvy shopper, this extends to the consumption of marketing messages behind branded content, influencers they follow, and brands they purchase from.

Content has adapted as consumers have shifted behaviours and become more conscious of the ethos's attached to products and brands they align with and their impacts on society.

SHANNON WALKER
The Evolution Of Creativity To Disrupt Change

Recognising their economic power, consumers are now voting for the type of world they want with their buying power whilst corporations shift their purpose, value proposition and marketing strategy to match the impending consumer demand.

As purposeful marketing has increasingly been on the rise, so have strategies to connect more meaningfully to audiences and better tailor messages to niche and segmented groups for greater relevance and resonance. In addition, content has reflected the consumer desire to see themselves and diverse groups represented in brand communication.

Studies have shown that 63% of consumers would like to see more diversity (Meta, 2021), 61% find it crucial in advertising, and 38% are more likely to trust brands that do well with showing diversity in their ads (Forbes, 2020). The more this practice is normalised, the faster we will move to a place where the notion of inclusive marketing will simply be known as marketing.

Real and relatable trumps popularity

A demand for relatable and authentic content has helped to democratise industries such as influencer marketing and change industry practices in advertising. "Real and relevant" has become more important for brands and their audiences than popularity. Therefore, brands have increasingly sought relationships with authentic voices to bring their brand messages to life that audiences can identify with.

As a result, both newly emerging and established brands have increasingly begun to partner with micro and nano influencers to create content that connects. The notion of "realness" has also impacted the creative methods marketers and influencers use, such as reduced airbrushing, photoshopping, misleading filters, and challenging notions of western ideals and beauty standards.

From Digitisation to Virtualisation

It would be remiss to discuss the future of content and influencer marketing without touching upon metaverse and how this will impact the industry, as well as conversations around body image, idealism, and inclusivity.

SHANNON WALKER
The Evolution Of Creativity To Disrupt Change

As digitalisation has introduced creative technology to enhance branded content, debates have heightened around social media personalities and how they represent their appearance on social media- mostly altered, faceted, and filtered.

With filters, skins and made-made virtual influencers and avatars being a key component of the metaverse, it poses the question: is the metaverse the solution to inclusive digital representation, or will it simply drive existing issues around equality, diversity, and inclusion (which we are nowhere near close to solving in the current world) in another realm? A glimmer of hope lies in the fact that, whilst the metaverse is around a decade from full fruition, there presents an opportunity for users, brands, and developers to build the type of space and content they want from scratch - embedding safeguarding, equality, and core values from its inception.

The future: Everyone deserves to feel seen, heard, empowered, inspired, and celebrated

Creativity is limitless; therefore, the industry will continue to innovate and evolve with technological advancements. However, the stories, representations, and narratives we tell through content will continue to have the same consequences if the same cycles and systems prevail and dominant groups and perspectives control and craft what content and the people in it look like.

As marketers, we must be continuously conscious of not repeating past mistakes and use our creative power to ensure content adds value to our communities, society, and the planet. We must think beyond the business benefits of conscious marketing and tap into our humanity, as everyone deserves to feel seen, heard, empowered, inspired, and celebrated. To ensure this lies in key fundamentals:

1. Hiring diverse core and extended teams
2. Working with broad creatives and talent
3. Making values a priority for all stakeholders that engage the brand
4. Immersion into different perspectives to better understand the communities you are marketing to
5. Developing campaigns/initiatives that positively impact communities, not solely market to them
6. Increased improvements on ways to make brand communication accessible for the disabled community

SHANNON WALKER
The Evolution Of Creativity To Disrupt Change

For the industry to continue to innovate and thrive, diversity and inclusion must be at the forefront of strategies, it must not be an exception but the norm, so content continues to heal wounds of the past, inspire change and be enjoyable for *all*.

Shannon Walker is a passionate and multi-disciplined creative communications professional and founder of Social Disruption a Digital PR and brand storytelling consultancy that specialises in supporting brands to shape purposeful and culturally rich communications. Shannon has enjoyed a 9 year career carving out a niche in the luxury consumer industry by disrupting traditional in-house PR environments and spearheading digital communication strategies that have led to triple percentage affiliate revenue growth and contributed to increased brand rankings. This disruptive spirit led her to work at prestigious businesses such as Liberty London where she launched the retailer's Influencer Engagement department, as well as work across KGA's portfolio of prestige fragrance brands which includes Cartier, Elie Saab, Issey Miyake and Jimmy Choo. As an advocate for inclusivity and diversity, Social Disruption is the vessel for the change Shannon wants to see in the industry. She has worked with emerging brands to leading corporations to offer a fresh perspective and support on the output of meaningful and Polycultural communications. Shannon is a member of the BCMA Influence Industry Steering Group.

SPERO PATRICIOS
Doing Good: Achieving Growth With Branded Content

Marketers globally are faced with the dual task of doing good while still achieving growth to create value for their business & their customers. But the question is, can they both be done successfully?

Growth is a focus of a company's strategy for success. The approach depends on the object of that growth. Profitability? Revenue? Market share? Each requires a different choice from the spectrum of brand and marketing plans.

Good, on the other hand, is both a business purpose/mission and a differentiator for the growth strategy. It's a prime ingredient infused into a marketing and content strategy, no matter what part of the growth spectrum the business pursues.

Can they both be done successfully?

Communicating a brand purpose and the practice of branded content are distinct but very much related. In some companies, the same brand content team might work on sustainability content, thought leadership, and educational content.

And some tactical content marketing plans rely heavily on a clear 'brand purpose' story that expresses itself as a content platform. *Airtel Touching Lives*[1] is a perfect example. Telecommunications services provider Airtel Nigeria, its commitment to empowering and uplifting vulnerable people, building communities, and creating value for all its stakeholders with its flagship CSR intervention, *Airtel Touching Lives*.

Airtel Touching Lives is a long-form branded content television reality show that seeks to offer practical relief, succour, hope, opportunities, and credible platforms to liberate and empower the underprivileged, disadvantaged, and hard-to-reach persons in society. The activities of the project are recorded and produced for national television to promote the spirit of giving, self-sacrifice, and love.

---
1 https://www.youtube.com/watch?v=T1uV-x7ev9E

SPERO PATRICIOS
Doing Good: Achieving Growth With Branded Content

Airtel Africa's Chief Executive Officer, Segun Ogunsanya, said a strong sense of purpose drives Airtel's relentless focus on sustainable initiatives that can positively impact its various communities.

Family accepting their new home from Airtel

According to Ogunsanya, the objective is powerful as it does not just define an individual or an entity but drives its every action and decision.

Nominee reaction after been awarded a new farming business

In 2001, Airtel procured its operating license, which is now being renewed.

SPERO PATRICIOS
Doing Good: Achieving Growth With Branded Content

It is possible to procure and renew an operating license, but you can only earn a social license. A social license is the love, loyalty, friendship and affection you get from the communities you operate and your different stakeholders.

While Airtel has renewed its operating license to provide telecommunications services, it is committed to its purpose of empowering and uplifting people and making a positive and lasting impact in the lives of its stakeholders, thereby earning its social license. To realise this vision, the *Airtel Touching Lives* initiative was created to offer relief and hope to the underprivileged and downtrodden and inspire the strong and the wealthy to support the vulnerable and the poor.

The Airtel Africa CEO also noted that *Airtel Touching Lives* would continue to focus on the program's overall philosophy while taking cognizance of critical events such as the global pandemic that has made life difficult for many people.

Airtel Touching Lives is a perfect example of doing good and achieving growth can exist together in a perfectly well-crafted branded content platform.

Spero Patricios is the Managing Director of Launch Factory, a leading brand experience agency based in Johannesburg. A recognised advertising heavyweight, Spero has been involved in the industry for over 30-years and created award-winning Television shows for multinational brands and accumulated numerous awards as well as becoming Greek Businessman of the Year which was awarded by ex-South African president Nelson Mandela. Spero is Chairman of BCMA South Africa and a member of the BCMA Global Council.

LAWRENCE RIBERO
Take The Risk

In my line of work, as an action director, I think a lot about risk everyday. It becomes part of your everyday thought process. What defines creative risk to you?

When I think of REAL risk, of putting everything on the line, I think of *Apocalypse Now* and *Psycho*. At those respective times, Coppola and Hitchcock were the most celebrated directors in Hollywood.

In both cases, the directors had to mortgage their homes to make these films. Why?

They believed in their vision. And they had the guts to go for it! To this day, these films have come to define Cinema.

Can we do the same in Branded Content?

When I think of risk in Branded Content, I think of the BMW films. Overall, it was considered a success in terms of results. YouTube hadn't been created yet, but it was Fincher at the helm calling the shots particularly on the second part. Twenty years later the films still work, and they still stand as a highwater mark for risk and achievement.

Robert Evans used to say, "you have to be a river boat gambler in this business". Times have changed...

Now we make creative choices with analytics and data and, as a result soul-less content.

I bet you can recall 3 to 5 of your favourite car chases off the top of your head? Which branded content campaigns have inspired you in the same way.

Individuality and a point of view are much rarer things, in today's marketplace of film, advertising and branded content.

LAWRENCE RIBERO
Take The Risk

If you've seen *Ford vs. Ferrari*, you'll remember the conversation that Matt Damon and Christian Bale have at the diner[1]. The real-life Ken Miles saw right through the charade. Both men were legends. Why?

Because they took risks…BUT there were opportunities within those risks. There are so many opportunities to just go for it!

If there's one thing I would encourage in the field of branded content is to 'just go for it'! Don't worry about what awards you might (or might not!) win, or what people may think of you. Create wonderment that is lasting. Create something with soul that will inspire. Show or develop individuality and take a risk or two and of course believe in yourself!

You'd be surprised what you could achieve if you aren't afraid to fail.

Lawrence Ribeiro is an award-winning Director who specialises in combining stunts, culture, movement and aesthetics forming Action Design & Content. He is the author of the book, The Unknown Art Of Driving. He has directed and shot well over 100 action sequences, from car chases and motorcycle stunts to fight sequences and has been mentored by the top stunt coordinators in the industry – Garrett Warren, Gary Powell and Andy Armstrong. His recent collaborations include editor extraordinaire Rick Pearson and Hollywood legend Doug Trumbull. Earlier in his career, he trained classically under well-known cinematographer Howard Wexler and Lane Leavitt, a top innovator in the stunt world. His love for action and the arts was fused in his unique upbringing. His father was a Navy frogman, professional rally driver and robotic engineer and his mother was a lover of all art forms. By the age of 21, he had traveled over 60,000 miles around the globe. His curiosity and quest for adventure led him to some of the most dangerous environments and jobs in the world, from heli-logging to mountain search and rescue in conflict zones. He has written the book, The Unknown Art of Driving, and is releasing his second book, Action 101 – A Guide to 2nd Unit/Action and the Arts. He has written for ICG, MovieMaker and Filmmaker Magazines and has given talks at the Art Center College of Design and at Film Independent, and currently serves on the Advisory Council for the Previsualization Society. In his free time, Lawrence enjoys treasure hunting, Native American mythology/culture, 1960s-1970s African-American culture, art appreciation, hiking and hockey.

---

1 https://www.youtube.com/watch?v=yL1dy1-AixM (clip starts at 1min 40secs)

KARNVIR MUNDREY
Navigating The Indian Content Marketing Jungle

With 1.4 billion people, 22 national languages, every major religion, the world's largest democracy and (post-covid) the fastest growing economy in the world – it is a content marketers dream.

But it's also a nightmare!

Content Marketing in India needs a deep understanding of the culture, traditions, and sensibilities of the people. And in a country with a highly participative and opinionated population – a slip of incorrect content can cause mass outrage!

But get it right and with a population size that is 1/6th of the world, you can bring great change, fantastic profits and even move the government!

The right use of content marketing has enabled the success of the Covid vaccination program - India has administered more than two billion Covid vaccination doses. Content marketing was extensively used to propagate mask use and vaccine acceptance.

So, what works and what doesn't in this diverse land?

Patriotism and celebration of Indian culture & traditions are evergreen content marketing genres - taking many forms. Like promoting the product that is 'Made in India', or the product being made with raw materials from India. It can also use colours, especially saffron, white, and green, to wake up the patriot in you. This usually happens every August, when brands start campaigning about independence and freedom, coinciding with India's Independence Day. In the same vein, celebrating the armed forces, their sacrifices and their hardships also creates great content success in India.

Indians are also an emotional society. And engaging with emotions always offers a long term connect with the target audience. Various brands have used this effectively. Tata Tea has aligned the energising virtue of tea, with a concept of 'Waking up' against injustice.

KARNVIR MUNDREY
Navigating The Indian Content Marketing Jungle

This famous phrase 'Jaago re' is the campaign aired by Tata tea. The campaign aims to change how people look at India. Their tagline goes like 'Chai piyo, soch badlo' which suggest that things be looked at from a different perspective.

Celebrating women's empowerment is another evergreen theme which is popular among Indian content marketers. India has a mixed history of women's rights and achievement. It has had women achievers in every field, and no restrictions in employment. However traditionally women have faced some glass ceilings and challenges to growth.

Content celebrating women's achievements are usually highly effective and have almost national appeal. India is working hard to change biases against age old taboos and bring equality of thought. Sanitary napkin brand Whisper launched a campaign "Touch the Pickle" – which was against the old age belief in certain societies that women during periods were "impure". Traditionally, especially in rural areas this has led to women sometimes being shunned during their menstruation days.

Campaigns which celebrate women or women achievers also have strong virality.

Bollywood – the Indian Film Industry - of course has long been a fantastic resource & a market for content marketing – Bollywood has never been afraid to try new things, especially when it comes to film marketing, because the wider the film's reach, the higher the box office receipts. Filmmakers have constantly taken innovative steps to get the most out of media, be it radio or television. And now it's dabbling into digital marketing, with the goal of going beyond likes and shares on social media. Filmmakers and actors are taking up newer and unique ways to promote their films and make it stand out amongst the crowd.

The promotion of a film starts much before the shooting commences. While post shoot marketing was more focused on in the earlier times, today filmmakers pay equal attention to both pre-shoot and post-shoot marketing of the film.

Now digital media, especially social media is being widely used to announce movies. In what appears to be a recent development, filmmakers are aiming at grand announcements through videos for upcoming movies.

KARNVIR MUNDREY
Navigating The Indian Content Marketing Jungle

Cricket is said to be a religion in India, not a sport – and the players are the Gods! Cricket like Bollywood offers a lot of opportunities and is the golden ticket to reach the masses. Creating content on cricket is usually popular, non-controversial and has mass appeal. Which makes it a strong tool to create effective content marketing campaigns.

Celebrating Indian traditions. With a rich heritage of thousands of years India offers a lot of content marketing opportunities that celebrate cherished moral values like respecting one's elders or lessons available through the many historic texts of India.

Humour is also another frequently used tool in content marketing. With India being a complex society and relatively high stress levels, humour has done brilliantly as a tool for content marketing – and often achieves quick virality. Again, with a sensitive society – humour needs to be handled carefully. Comedians have been known to be sued by people who found their humour repulsive or not agreeable.

Increasingly however religion is now a sensitive topic and in the complex social structure of India, anything that is religion-centric can hit sensitivities. Even though the Surf Excel 'Dag Acche Hai' TVC was centred around religious harmony, it instantly faced criticism from several quarters.

The Future? It's probably going to get even more complex. A strong understanding of Indian culture and sensitivities will likely create stories of success!

Karnvir Mundrey is the Chief Ideation Officer at Atharva Marcom. His journey in content started over two decades ago in the era of 2.4 kbps modems, when he assisted in creating one of the earliest Bulletin Board Systems (BBS) – in a pre-internet era. In the past he has been on all sides of the content ocean – be it print, electronic or digital. He was part of the editorial team at PC World India – India's most popular technology publication, and engaged with global technology brands like Microsoft, Oracle, Yahoo, amongst others. His series of research papers, titled 'Strategic Web Marketing', were one of the first to explore concepts such as Return On Investment in the digital space. He is often featured in the media, for his views on the industry, and is on various committees of industry and commerce. He is a post graduate from the London School of Economics & Political Science (LSE), and is currently based in Bangalore, India. Karnvir is President of BCMA India and a member of the BCMA Global Council.

DR. SEVIL YESILOGLU
Future Trends Of Influencer Marketing: Virtual Versus In-House

In the dynamic field of marketing communications brands are constantly investigating methods of consumer communications across rapidly developing digital media platforms. As marketers and advertisers explore (or measure) how consumers engage with peers and friends when seeking brand or product related information, they are beginning to seek track and develop new alternatives for peer-to-peer brand and product related digital communications.

When considering human-to-human brand or product-related interactions, we imagine influencers with marketing strategies built entirely upon the word-of-mouth economy.

However, as online advertising becomes less obvious as advertising, we are beginning to see new trends in influencer marketing practice: virtual and in-house influencers are becoming key marketing trends.

New levels of hybrid in-person and virtual interaction have been made possible by advancements in connectivity and digitalisation. Consequently, we are witnessing the emergence of virtual influencers as digital avatars created by a wide range of multimedia technology platforms.

Using graphical illustrations and representations of characters in place of individual human influencers is increasingly popular among brands, marketers and consumers. These virtual influencers are seen as a bridge between real and digital worlds offering additional amusement or a means of escaping[1].

Their success can be measured by how expertly they are scripted, their narrative potential, and how successfully they connect with both their fans and the brands they represent[2]. Their unique storylines are found to be great service of escapism for consumers.

---

1 Arsenyan, J. and Mirowska, A., 2021. Almost human? A comparative case study on the social media presence of virtual influencers. International Journal of Human-Computer Studies, 155, p.102694.

2 Moustakas, E., Lamba, N., Mahmoud, D. and Ranganathan, C., 2020, June. Blurring lines between fiction and reality: Perspectives of experts on marketing effectiveness of virtual influencers. In 2020 International Conference on Cyber Security and Protection of Digital Services (Cyber Security) (pp. 1-6). IEEE.

DR. SEVIL YESILOGLU
Future Trends Of Influencer Marketing:
Virtual Versus In-House

Comparable to game characters or avatars, virtual influencers help their followers to create imaginative world that help them to get further entertainment[3].

Virtual influencers are designed to share constantly positive messaging and make fewer obvious mistakes. However, this can lead to questions about their sense of authenticity by marketing professionals.

Brands and corporations are also beginning to develop and establish influencer teams within their organisations. These in-house influencers are directed by marketing teams who manage individual influencers, develop targets and measure influencer impact on consumer purchasing journeys across all aspects of marketing campaigns.

In-house teams typically focus on understanding the influencer marketing landscape, identifying key personalities and ensuring content strategy is aligned with companies' values and mission statements.

Brands like Nike, Pretty Little Thing and Mars run their influencer marketing campaigns in-house to build enduring relationships in long-term partnerships. Taking a strategic approach to developing these relationships provides huge productivity advantages for their businesses.

With advancing changes in consumers' requirements for brand communications, these two trends in influencer marketing practices offer exciting marketing opportunities for both brands and consumers.

Dr Sevil Yesiloglu is the Course Leader for BA (Hons) Advertising at London College of Communication (LCC). Sevil is Associate Fellow HEA and enthusiastic lecturer bringing research led teaching into the classroom to help students gain critical analysis skills as well as practical skills within digital advertising discipline. Sevil's research covers digital aspects of advertising including online harms, brand related content, influencer marketing and social media usage. Her first edited book covers influencer marketing which investigate different elements of brand community building and engagement (Routledge 2020). Sevil gained her PhD at Bournemouth university thesis titled: 'To post or not to post: Examining motivations of brand/product-related posts on Social Networking Sites'.

---

[3] Luger, E., Sellen, A., 2016. Like having a really bad PA": the gulf between user expectation and experience of conversational agents. In: Proceedings of the 2016 CHI Conference on Human Factors in Computing Systems, pp. 5286–5297. https://doi.org/10.1145/2858036.2858288.

DR. SEVIL YESILOGLU
Future Trends Of Influencer Marketing: Virtual Versus In-House

This famous phrase 'Jaago re' is the campaign aired by Tata tea. The campaign aims to change how people look at India. Their tagline goes like 'Chai piyo, soch badlo' which suggest that things be looked at from a different perspective.

Celebrating women's empowerment is another evergreen theme which is popular among Indian content marketers. India has a mixed history of women's rights and achievement. It has had women achievers in every field, and no restrictions in employment. However traditionally women have faced some glass ceilings and challenges to growth.

Content celebrating women's achievements are usually highly effective and have almost national appeal. India is working hard to change biases against age old taboos and bring equality of thought. Sanitary napkin brand Whisper launched a campaign "Touch the Pickle" – which was against the old age belief in certain societies that women during periods were "impure". Traditionally, especially in rural areas this has led to women sometimes being shunned during their menstruation days.

Campaigns which celebrate women or women achievers also have strong virality.

Bollywood – the Indian Film Industry - of course has long been a fantastic resource & a market for content marketing – Bollywood has never been afraid to try new things, especially when it comes to film marketing, because the wider the film's reach, the higher the box office receipts. Filmmakers have constantly taken innovative steps to get the most out of media, be it radio or television. And now it's dabbling into digital marketing, with the goal of going beyond likes and shares on social media. Filmmakers and actors are taking up newer and unique ways to promote their films and make it stand out amongst the crowd.

The promotion of a film starts much before the shooting commences. While post shoot marketing was more focused on in the earlier times, today filmmakers pay equal attention to both pre-shoot and post-shoot marketing of the film.

Now digital media, especially social media is being widely used to announce movies. In what appears to be a recent development, filmmakers are aiming at grand announcements through videos for upcoming movies.

HAEM ROY
Here, There And Everywhere

How can you expand your thinking to build a truly omnichannel branded content strategy?

Great news! You have a well-produced, entertaining piece of branded content ready to you. And it ticks all the boxes when it comes to good content, and seamless brand inclusion.

That is just the beginning.

That stellar piece of content you have created is as good as invisible if it is not backed by the right media strategy. I remember reading somewhere "…put 30% of the effort and money behind creating content, and 70% behind making sure it reaches the right people".

Alright, so now you know that you need a good media plan. Adding in a little bit of everything however is not the trick here. Start with understand the end goal – what do you want people watching this content to think and do? Know that you have the best flavour of chips in the country? Talk about it to everyone they know? Make sure every time they go to the store, they look at the chips? Remember that you are more than just any other brand of chips and that you care for the planet? Zero in on ONE objective – too many will dilute your plan and reduce effectiveness. Let's presume it is about a 'chip that cares'. And let's presume your branded content is a series of videos about heroes in the community that cared and brought change through action.

Now start with making sure you have a media plan that reaches the audience that cares about caring. Are they on Instagram? Do they watch TV? Do they watch TV while scrolling Instagram? Tick off the boxes and build a plan that indexes high with the right audience.

Next thing is taking the piece of content and tying it with action. So, your consumer has seen it. It is time to make them remember it and drive them to action. In this case, how about asking them to join a petition that is very focused on the community, tangible, and not vague?

HAEM ROY
Here, There And Everywhere

Rally the consumers to join the cause. BUT - and this is critical - don't do it just for lip service. Make it real. Make it happen. Only do this if you do care. Because believe it or not, consumers can spot a fake.

So, good content - check, reaching the right audience at the right platform – check, action – check. Lastly, momentum and layering.

Layer the strategy with smaller pieces of content, messaging, and media. One and done is rarely ever good enough. Can it be Behind the scenes shots? Could it be beach clean-up events where your brand gets to engage with consumers 1-on-1? Tips on what people can do to show they care. Offers that tie back the main message of caring to driving purchase. Keep the momentum going because it is easy to forget and move on. And keep it consistent with smaller strategies that do not need a heavy lift, but still fit with the overall branded content concept.

And there you have it. You have now expanded your thinking to build a truly omnichannel branded content strategy. And you have expanded the impact of that one piece of content, taking it much further.

Haem Roy is Senior Branded Content Manager at Rogers Sports & Media in Toronto, Canada. Haem is a Branded Content and Integrations leader, a Creative Strategist and Omnichannel Marketer. She has worked on both the creative as well as the business side, leading on all aspects of strategy, content creation, pitching, execution, marketing & optimisation. Not only has Haem worked on custom series for major brands such as Unilever, Mercedes Benz but she has also led & built marketing teams. A speaker & panellist, she co-hosts the BCMA Canada Candid chats series and actively advocates for diversity & inclusion. Haem is part of a Toronto-based improvisational comedy troupe 'Eyesore'. Haem is President of BCMA Canada and a member of the BCMA Global Council.

DANIEL SÁNCHEZ
Does Your Brand Have What It Takes To Make An Authentic Connection?

Over the past few years, we've witnessed a powerful consumer preference shift: trust in brands is at an all-time low[1] and companies are scrambling to 'get real' by nurturing their relationships with customers through authentic marketing strategies. While we know that authenticity will be the new buzzword, it's important to explore what this looks like both when managing your campaign and measuring its performance.

The Scramble for Authenticity

Consumer trust had been on the decline for years, but the Covid-19 pandemic truly cast a new light on these issues. In a way, it was a perfect storm: global brands were suddenly unable to get their products into the hands of those who needed them while increasingly coming under scrutiny for their roles in everything we deem to be wrong with society.

To counter this, companies must make smart decisions about the partnerships they form with content creators, and, by extension, their followers. Here's a roundup of trends we expect to grow in the future of influencer marketing.

Let your products speak for themselves

Millennials and Gen Zers are digital natives, and as such are adept at seeing through even the most carefully designed 'authentic' ads. The solution? Letting go of the idea that all communication should be brand controlled and making room for conversation; monologues are being transformed into dialogues.

What does this mean for your campaigns? We see this as giving influencers the freedom to say what they really think about your product. Any negative feedback should be addressed from the bottom up, not just superficially.

---

1 https://www.multivu.com/players/English/8736051-2020-gustavson-brand-trust-index/

DANIEL SÁNCHEZ
Does Your Brand Have What It Takes To Make An Authentic Connection?

This responsiveness is at the core of any authentic marketing strategy. Of course, this confidence doesn't come overnight. Influencers should feel comfortable discussing these issues with the brand, something that brings us to our next point: the importance of establishing solid, long-term relationships with your influencers.

Foster ongoing partnerships

It is already a noted trend that brands will look for long-term partnerships[2] instead of one-off deals. This approach acknowledges that users require multiple touchpoints with your product to convert, and brand awareness is not established by one flashy sponsored post. Additionally, it comes down to the fact that 'buy-in' sells. An influencer who has developed a relationship with a brand and reflects its values will transmit this sentiment to their followers. And how do you achieve this buy-in? Forming a relationship is a good way to start.

Nowadays, Influencer Relationship Management (IRM) tools[3] offer a way to measure an influencer's metrics and seamlessly pursue a relationship with them, all from one platform. A good IRM will allow you to integrate your email to keep track of all brand communications with your content creator.

Additionally, many allow you to add notes to jot down info about influencers' preferences, sizing information – whatever you need! Saving this relevant contact, communication, and personal information is key to making sure your relationship starts off on the right track and remains fruitful for years to come.

Soft metrics for measuring authenticity

So we know that a successful marketing campaign goes beyond just looking at the main Key Performance Indicators (KPIs) like the number of followers, interactions, and engagement. Now, the question is how to measure influencer authenticity and their performance in your new, authentic campaigns.

Putting a value on authenticity is not easy, but it'll be worth the trouble. Here are some of our ideas for how authenticity can be measured to help you choose the best influencer for your campaign:

---

2 https://influencermarketinghub.com/influencer-marketing-trends/
3 https://knowledge.influencity.com/irm/what-is-an-irm

Does Your Brand Have What It Takes To Make An Authentic Connection?

- **Insight into influencer interests and brand affinity** gives an idea of an influencer's ideals as well as the content they consume and post. Well-aligned interests are key to authentic influencer marketing
- **Insight into audience interests and brand affinity** introduces you to their follower community. If an influencer shows an interest in a socially responsible campaign but their audience insights suggest that their followers may not be receptive to this, then perhaps this isn't the ideal collaboration for your brand
- **Measuring comment sentiment** harnesses the power of AI to "read" through a creator's comments section. This will tell you how an influencer is perceived
- **The number of sponsored vs. organic posts** in an influencer's recent posts. If you see #ad after #ad, expect consumers to lose trust in this content creator. Now that countries are cracking down on endorsements[4], it's more important than ever to choose your influencers wisely
- **Follower quality** indicates if your content reaches real people who may be interested in your product or service, or just a group of bots[5]. A good IRM tool will divide followers into those who are useful to you, and those who are not
- **Audience reachability** predicts if your sponsored content will be seen by your key demographic or get lost among the thousands of other accounts that they follow. Get the best bang for your buck by focusing on influencers with smaller audiences, ensuring that your content is seen

The Rise of Performance-based Campaigns

Once an authentic connection has been established, it's time to put it to work, ideally across different channels. As mentioned before, native ads have the most impact when a degree of brand awareness is established. Exceptional growth will be the reward for companies who are able to identify the best-performing content, multiple this across channels, and amplify this impact with well-targeted paid strategies.

To see this strategy in action, say you're collaborating with an influencer for a campaign on Instagram, TikTok, and YouTube. To do this, you'll need an IRM that can tell you this influencer's current metrics on these platforms, the performance of your campaigns on each one, and how much of your budget you've invested in each.

---

[4] https://www.ftc.gov/system/files/documents/plain-language/1001a-influencer-guide-508_1.pdf
[5] https://www.cloudflare.com/en-gb/learning/bots/what-is-a-social-media-bot/

DANIEL SÁNCHEZ
Does Your Brand Have What It Takes To Make An Authentic Connection?

This network-level data is key for determining your Return on Investment (ROI). Out of a total campaign, how much interaction can be attributed to TikTok vs. YouTube? Can you identify factors that explain this difference? Perhaps your TikTok publications were better timed and resonated more highly with viewers. What can you learn from your TikTok campaign that you can apply to future YouTube content?

The Rise of Social Commerce

Established brands and new start-ups alike are rushing to engage shoppers who are increasingly spending time online. This strategy pays, as exemplified by Shopify's $2.9 billion[6] in sales on Black Friday 2021. Of this figure, 72% of sales were made on mobile devices. It should come as no surprise, therefore, that brands are projected to spend a whopping $16.4 billion[7] on influencer marketing over the course of 2022. According to this same study, over 75% of brands intend to dedicate part of their budget to influencer marketing in 2022. Of those who already have a strategy in place, 68% intend to increase their existing budget.

As budgets grow, so do the features that social networks offer for their content creators, indicating a professionalisation of the sector. Influencers are now expected to be true thought leaders and have the tools at their disposal to become so:

- **Instagram 'guides'** - allow creators to add content with commentary, like a sort of mini-blog. This new feature requires influencers to pinpoint the content their followers want to consume and curate it. The result is social commerce: where social networks and online sales meet
- **Direct-sales tools** - eliminate the friction from transactions and directly attributes sales to specific creators. Creators are no longer expected to just drive awareness, conversions are now solidly in their hands as well
- **Live Rooms** - essentially democratize panel sessions and talk shows by allowing creators to host up to 3 guests in live sessions held directly from the Instagram app, no auditorium or recording studio needed

---

6 https://investors.shopify.com/news-and-events/press-releases/news-details/2021/Black-Friday-but-Make-It-Epic-Shopify-Merchants-Break-Records-with-2.9-Billion-in-Sales/default.aspx

7 https://influencermarketinghub.com/influencer-marketing-benchmark-report/

DANIEL SÁNCHEZ
Does Your Brand Have What It Takes To Make An Authentic Connection?

- **Pinned comments** - a useful tool for up-and-coming thought leaders. Creators can pin the insights they want to associate with a post and therefore guide the narrative

Daniel Sánchez is the Co-Founder and CEO of Influencity. Daniel started his career as a tech consultant for one of the most world prestigious consulting firms, even before starting his degree as a Software Engineer. Has worked and lived abroad in Australia, Germany, UK, Ireland, Spain, the US, among others. He founded Influencity, in 2014 which is now considered the most complete AI-powered Influencer Marketing platform for worldwide brands & agencies with over 170M influencers. Daniel is a member of the BCMA Influence Industry Steering Group.

---

8 https://sproutsocial.com/insights/instagram-features/

ÁLVARO BERMÚDEZ DE CASTRO
Content With Purpose

The advertising landscape is constantly changing; it always has been, but there are factors that demonstrate the current and vertiginous transformation of traditional formulas to connect both brands and media with their audiences. For the media today, it is more relevant than ever before to generate and incorporate quality content to their grids; in order to allow competition with more and better content. Bringing brands into this equation is the perfect formula for both parties.

One of the characteristics that define the evolution of communication today is the incorporation of the values and ethics of companies as generators of trust, credibility and commitment. They favour engagement and serve as an activation lever for the generation of business and purchase decisions. Brands are becoming increasingly aware of this reality and responding with agility to the new demands of their stakeholders.

At WPP (the company to which GroupM belongs to) we detected this promising social and business change some time ago, and declared that our purpose would be to 'Use the power of creativity and media to build a better future for our society, planet, customers and communities'.

To realise this purpose, for 15-years we have had Motion Content Group (MCG), the group's content creation company from which we finance, develop, produce, and distribute premium content. We invest in content in partnership with the world's leading talents, producers, networks, and platforms, all aimed at tomorrow's consumers - the emerging generation - who demand responsibility to be taken from companies and brands.

We work across all genres, with a flexible approach and numerous investment models and ways of working. Each agreement is structured according to both the needs of our partners and market conditions. We do this to support their creative and commercial needs, while attaining value and creating opportunities for WPP and GroupM agencies and clients.

ÁLVARO BERMÚDEZ DE CASTRO
Content With Purpose

In fact, we have been managing our carbon footprint for the past 15-years, reducing emissions every year since 2006, although we recognise the need to accelerate the pace of change. To drive this, the group amended its statement of purpose to make our commitment to the planet explicit, as an integral part of our business.

We formalised these principles and created the 'Responsible Investment Framework', which covers brand safety, data ethics, DEI, responsible journalism, and sustainability; our shared values are clear.

Rationale for change

WPP's statement leaves no room for doubt: we define ourselves as a creative company that uses the power of creativity and media to build a better future for our people, clients and communities. As Mark Read, CEO of WPP, states: "the work we do has the power to bring about change".

Christian Juhl, Global CEO of GroupM, goes further and declares that "brands must allocate more media budgets to achieve positive social and environmental impact" and Kirk McDonald, GroupM North America CEO states that: "As the world's largest media network, it is our responsibility to help clients allocate media budgets as a force for good, and we are using our scale to achieve positive and meaningful change".

These statements, expressed by global leaders in our network, make us reflect on MCG's contribution to make these intentions tangible. We are convinced that from the media and relevant content, we can contribute significantly.

Film, TV, and digital content have the power to change opinions and behaviours, scaling up a more sustainable and equitable future. We connect entertainment with media and advertising to create value and opportunities for our partners and advertisers worldwide.

At MCG, we firmly believe that impactful content can help change the world for the better, and we are guided by simple, overarching principles. The easiest way to understand the values we support is by empowering a wider range of people to tell their stories, allowing quieter and smaller voices to be heard, and enabling people to learn from the experience of others.

ÁLVARO BERMÚDEZ DE CASTRO
Content With Purpose

Positive Impact

At MCG we have strived to find a way to help tell the stories that resonate with our audiences and help us create real and sustainable change. Positive Impact is aimed at creative positive change in the areas of diversity, equity and inclusion (DEI) and sustainability. Developed in collaboration with GroupM's agencies and clients, the funding initiative will support stories - premium documentaries, high-end TV series, landmark series and films - that truly inspire positive change in society.

To further ground any initiative along these lines, for the BCMA we have created a specific working commission to strengthen Branded Content actions with purpose[1].

The objective of this Commission is to both promote Branded Content as an ideal tool for the active communication of Brand Purpose - given the relevance it provokes in the audience - and to encourage a consistent use of the former with the Sustainable Development objectives of companies.

There is a lot of work to be done. Many of us are convinced that these types of initiatives are the ones that will make it possible for changes to truly permeate society and for companies to be perceived as something real and possible.

Álvaro Bermúdez de Castro is Managing Director Content & Product at GroupM Spain and VP of treasury at BCMA Spain. With a degree in Economic Sciences from the Complutense University of Madrid, Álvaro has more than 20-years of experience in the advertising market, marketing and commercial departments of different TV networks and exclusive media. In 2008 he joined Mindshare as Director of Performance. He previously was part of the Brand Entertainment department at Initiative Media for 4-years. He currently leads the Innovation and Content area of Mindshare Spain, offering creative solutions and Branded Content, developing Entertainment formats, including sports Marketing and Sponsorship projects, establishing greater differentiation and notoriety for brands. Álvaro has been a member of the BCMA Research and Measurement Commission since 2016.

---

1 https://bcma.es/comision-de-branded-content-con-proposito/

ADAM KACZMARSKI
The Power of Branded Content Production

What is most important for a brand that wishes to commission branded content (and for the purposes of this essay I'll mainly refer to longform broadcast quality content, because that's what we make at Electric Robin) is to ask themselves, 'Why am I doing this?'

So, the obvious things first. The purpose of branded content/brand funded programming is to do what any good story should do, which is illicit an emotional response in its audience. When done properly, it should make the viewer feel something that is consistent with the brand's own values.

When asked to name my favourite/most powerful examples of 'branded content' there are two examples that stand out.

The first is the *Guinness Book of Records*, first published in 1955 after the Managing Director of the famous drinks company attended a shoot (guns, not cameras). During proceedings, a passionate debate took place within the party, concerning whether the golden plover or the red grouse was the fastest game bird in Europe.

Realising there was no existing reference book that contained the answer, Sir Hugh Beaver commissioned The Guinness Book of (superlatives and now) Records. A thousand copies of the original run were printed and given away to pubs as a branded marketing freebie. Demand grew for extra copies, and it would go on to be a festive bestseller.

While the book carries the company name, it makes no mention of the price, flavour, or superior quality of a certain black and white stout. But Guinness's association with the concept (and the subsequent spin offs – TV shows, live shows, museums, websites, video games etc) is so strong that despite being sold by Diageo in 2001 it continues to carry the original brand's name. What started as the result of an argument in a pub (and let's be honest, what great ideas don't?) and a smart marketing giveaway idea grew to be the world's foremost authority on amazing achievements, a standalone brand worth $65m when sold.

ADAM KACZMARSKI
The Power of Branded Content Production

Secondly, there's the *Michelin Guide*, where in 1900 a tyre company decided to give away 35,000 copies of their guide to the best restaurants and inns around France, all at a time when there were fewer than 3,000 cars on the roads. The plan was not only to grow awareness of their own company, but to help further a burgeoning automobile industry, which would serve to increase the overall demand for travel, cars and, accordingly, car tyres. For 20-years, these guides would be distributed free until their popularity was such that they had built an audience, meaning the company could monetise the idea.

Fast forward a century and this piece of lateral thinking spawned a reference guide that is recognised worldwide as the gold standard for fine dining...all from a brand whose main business is the production of rubber tyres.

Michelin are a premium brand so perhaps being an authority of fine dining helps legitimise a higher price point of its tyres? An emotional connection among those 'in the know' who will insist that their vehicles are fitted with Michelin above Pirelli, Bridgestone or Nexen?

There are intangibles that accompany bold ideas, such as those that see the traditional marketing rulebook thrown from the car window before speeding off (probably towards a charming little bistro) and leaving it in the dust.

For me, the two examples above demonstrate that:

> a) Both concepts started as free branded 'give-aways' that gradually built their own audience before eventually becoming valuable and prestigious brands in their own right.

> b) It is not appropriate to measure branded content by the same metrics used for standard marketing. Yet since there's a creative/media agency, marketing department and numerous degrees of post campaign analysis involved, as opposed to fewer standardised measuring tools for brand funded content pieces of longform or native content, the venture often falls victim to the same reporting metrics as TVCs or even digital advertising. This is not a valid comparison.

Would a bold idea such as *Guinness Book of Records* or the *Michelin Guide* have a chance of making it beyond a brainstorming session in today's ROI-driven world?

ADAM KACZMARSKI
The Power of Branded Content Production

Whatever your opinion, it is crucial to separate the power of branded content ideas from standard advertising metrics. Content of this nature requires different metrics – either alongside original programmes of a similar budget launching on the same platform at the same timeslot, or experiential/PR campaigns that have much more limited reach, but whose purpose is to illicit a higher emotional reaction and brand affinity. Branded content is more nuanced than an ad campaign, and nearly often necessitates input from other stakeholders such as those representing the platform as well as the producers.

Making powerful brand funded content

In 2019/20, production company Electric Robin teamed up with AB InBev and the team at StoryLab (a Dentsu company) to develop an entertainment programme format, *Beer Masters*, that would change consumer's perceptions of their entire industry. They wanted a series that elevated the art of brewing, demonstrating how skilled and difficult a process it is to make consistently great beer. This was the purpose of the show rather than focussing on one specific brand of beer in their portfolio.

Already, this was a bold step to take given the huge amount of ambition involved with a brand 'owning' their industry category. It is why traditional content formats can be tremendously broad – travel, property, cooking, DIY, etc. – but individual brands within those verticals might, understandably, wonder what the value of investing in a project is if their own brand is not the sole focal point, with the added possibility of their competitors 'riding the wave' of their investment.

By way of insuring themselves against this, content producers are inevitably asked by the brands to ensure a set number of identifiable 'brand moments'. Our view is that these moments should always be an intrinsic part of the overall narrative and tone of what is being produced.

Instances that are a representation of the brand should be as much about the cinematography, colour palate, music, scripting, casting, content of the show as it is putting a bottle of beer, a watch, or an aeroplane into a scene. Why? Well, it is worth considering what would be most important to the viewer. Is it being engrossed in a story/format that has been developed for months and engaged by the handsomely paid on-screen talent (carefully selected after multiple rounds of research to ensure they themselves are 'on brand')?

ADAM KACZMARSKI
The Power of Branded Content Production

Or is it the bottle they are holding holding/phone handset they are using/wristwatch they are wearing/aeroplane they are flying in? Viewers can sniff out contrived moments a mile off, and they will rarely enhance engagement with the show when the point is to absorb and enjoy its purpose – i.e., that which conveys the virtues and ethos of the brand in ways that traditional advertising cannot.

If the audience are really focused on brand visibility, perhaps the content itself is not actually that engaging. If you really want a product or service to be front and centre of the scene, perhaps it would have been wiser creating a 30-second advert or billboard poster. Content and narrative needs to be the primary focus if you are to get the most from the endeavour.

Economic realities dictate that branded content (which comes with a relatively high cost) cannot solely be a passion project – there must be some tangible results that work for the business. This is where communication between client, production company and creative agency are key - we always try to ensure that we collaborate with all parties to maximise efficiencies and create supplementary content that can be used as part of a much broader campaign.

The principal content - which engages, entertains, or changes perceptions on a macro level - should be combined with specific messaging about a product's quality, value for money, sustainability, durability etc. - which are key messages for a TVC or billboard but unsuitable for a piece of longform content. To put it another way: the most powerful brand funded travel series would inspire and amaze the viewer with how fascinating far-flung corner of Planet Earth are and awaken a spirit of adventure and wanderlust within them. It doesn't need to tell you how much it costs to get there and which airports to fly from – that's a job that should be done by auxiliary content and a supporting campaign; and I think that brands are in a fortunate position given the availability of technology and targeted advertising solutions, which can more closely align the ideology of a brand content project to more specific calls to action.

The heaviest lifting always happens in the initial stages prior to life off. That's when the brand must invest the most thought and when a variety of questions need addressing before cameras roll. For instance, handsome fees aside, there's often a job to convince talent (on-screen and off) to take a step into the unknown with an unproven format. But once you have that 1st example/series there will always be something tangible to build on and develop.

ADAM KACZMARSKI
The Power of Branded Content Production

Being first to market and having ownership of original IP (rather than badging an existing format) can allow for bolder and more exciting activations (books, live events, pop-up stores, apps & games etc.) in the future. But these need time and patience to develop naturally - as they would do for any new format.

So many briefs from brands taking their first steps into long-form content creation come with the tagline – *"We want to make the Great British Bake Off of (insert product category)"* - which is a testament to that show and the fact that for the UK market it is considered by so many to be a showstopper of format development success.

Reading between the lines, what those briefs often mean is "I want to fast forward to something that looks like *Great British Bake Off* as it is right now - after 12 series. With over a decade of work building an audience and developing format points, a prime-time slot on a major broadcaster, inspired presenter combinations and occupying a place in people's heart's just next to Sir David Attenborough."

What they probably do not want is the show's first series, when Mary Berry and Paul Hollywood (both inspired castings that a seasoned commissioner knew would work beautifully while a marketeer might immediately dismiss for not having a large enough Instagram following) joined Mel and Sue on the road each week in locations such as Melton Mowbray and Sandwich, before the series grew an audience and the format was tweaked so that the contestants ended up inside the giant white tent.

To summarise then, I think that if there's a 'power' in branded content production, it lies in believing in the longevity and taking ownership of a strong initial idea that can evolve alongside the brand's own philosophy and business objectives for series 2,3…12 etc. Of course, that also benefits production companies, but if the purpose isn't to create something memorable, that can endure and provide a strong legacy, then is it worth doing? Why collaborate with a company whose day job is in developing longform content and formats, if that isn't the end goal?

If well executed, Brand Funded Programming can both 'give back' to the audience by entertaining them, but also be woven into a traditional targeted advertising campaign that the brand would create anyway – thus having a multiplier effect. Much like brewing a great beer you can have the all the necessary elements thrown together, but the process requires time, patience, compromise and above all else, trust.

ADAM KACZMARSKI
The Power of Branded Content Production

And so there must be an understanding that owned properties such as a content series take time to properly ferment and might not necessarily deliver overnight results.

The *Guinness Book of Records* and *Michelin Guide* examples demonstrate that given time marketing ideas originating from brands have the power to become so much more – an annual stocking filler people worldwide are happy to give/receive or a globally recognised standard for supreme culinary quality and hospitality.

Beer Masters, produced by Electric Robin, funded by AB InBev shown on Prime Video

Today's (and tomorrow's) equivalent might be the audience setting the EPG to record a brand funded series or downloading a mobile game a brand has created.

But success will always be dictated by how authentic and engaging the content is and how much focus is put on thinking 'audience and story first', rather than with the brand in mind.

With *Beer Masters* we were able to develop a show that was among the most popular originals viewed on the Amazon Prime platform that year, was distributed into European markets, achieving an 8/10 rating from viewers on IMDB...but we also created a show that succeeded in increasing perceptions of quality, favourability and purchase intent for the brands featured.

ADAM KACZMARSKI
The Power of Branded Content Production

We hope it's a great case study for the power of branded content productions and we look forward to creating many more as the industry evolves.

Adam Kaczmarski is Creative Producer at Electric Robin (a Banijay Company). Adam is an award-winning creative content producer working in the UK and International markets. He has developed content for major sports sponsorships and activations, as well as creating Advertiser Funded Programming (AFP) and Branded Content. He has been involved with format development and project management for high profile productions. His accolades include, Campaign Big Awards 2019 - Best Branded Content - Freddie v Freddie, Kinsale Shark 2019; Media Week Gold Award 2012 (Media Idea - Launch) for ESPN/Budweiser FA Cup Campaign.

PROFESSOR IAIN MACRURY
Branded Content And Long-Form Semiotics: The Case Of Snackmasters

"Diversification", "fragmentation", "convergence", "disruption", "digitalisation". Media is front of mind today when we think about promotional communications. Rightly so. But 'content' does not look after itself. The medium is not the (only) message. A message-focus, highlighting what the content says or seeks to say to, or to do for, its audience, remains crucial. Semiotics provides a staple tool in the repertoire of approaches available to us when we take a perspective preoccupied with the 'message' or 'content' aspect of promotional communication—focusing on what it means and *how* it means.

So, to add to thinking about branded content, I want to set out impressions of an episode of a UK TV format broadcast on Channel 4, *Snackmasters*. I consider it exemplary. In an early episode in season 2 (episode 2)[1], *Snackmasters* applied its format to Domino's Pizza. In particular, I want to use this *Snackmasters* example to help think about the continuing relevance of semiotic analysis in the field of branded content.

Semiotics – a tool for critical reflection

Semiotics, originally a mid-century academic-scholarly preoccupation associated with structuralism, gained traction in the 1980s (Levy 1987; Williamson 1978; Noth 1988) within promotional communication industries - especially brand consulting and advertising (Lury and Warde 1997). But, can semiotics stay relevant today?[2] As promotional formats shift from highly structured formats (ads, packaging, logos) to include more 'open' and discursive longer-form narrative communications characteristic of branded content, can traditional semiotics apply?

This question arises, in part, from a misconception about semiotics. Scholars and practitioners need not typecast semiotics and see it solely applicable to bounded small-scale texts like posters or TV ads. Such presumption is not unexpected.

---

1 December 2022 and streaming ever since on All4
2 There is a continuing academic and practitioner interest in semiotics for promotional communications. See Lawes (2002; 2020 and Oswald 2012)

PROFESSOR IAIN MACRURY
Branded Content And Long-Form Semiotics: The Case Of Snackmasters

Most students first encounter semiotics in the classic texts of the discipline as applied to such examples. Many of us will know great examples of using semiotics for fashion, perfume or car ads (Williamson 1978; Danesi 2018; MacRury 2009). But this is a foreclosure of the adaptability of this approach. The underlying tenor of semiotic theory provides an orientation to the world (and its 'texts') that recognises signification all around us. Semiotics "in the wild" helps explore processes underpinning 'open systems' of signification, meaning-making, exchange and sense-making (Lotman 1990).

Semiotics has applications across media and non-media environments, from digital pop-up ads to blockbuster movies to sunset landscape vistas. Its conceptions help us to make better, or at least more structured, sense of any form of communication (intentional or otherwise). It is part terminology, part ordinary intuition. Reacknowledging the broad applicability of semiotic ideas reminds us that semiotic processes associated with closed, simple example texts (such as advertisements) are also at work within longer-form communications. Branded content films, branded entertainments, or YouTube influencer spiels offer cases in point.

The Rhetoric of Domino's

The *Snackmasters* Domino's episode offers a dramatic instance. I chose this because it correlates very closely with the seminal text in advertising semiotics, Roland Barthes's 1964 piece on The Rhetoric of the Image (Barthes 1977). Those familiar with Barthes's essay will recall a dense and theoretically thoughtful articulation of a process of meaning transfer applied to a print ad - the "rhetorical" mobilisation of visual imagery (signifiers) in the composition of an influential advertising sign – for Pasta. The ad (and Barthes's essay) brought Panzani pasta to life on the page.

Barthes showed how advertising signification builds associations between a brand name and a series of assembled images and sounds; the result is the visually alluring substantiation of an idea, a rhetorical proposition about what the Panzani brand might mean to its audiences. In his case, the ad underlines and authenticates Panzani's claim to natural-organic Italian heritage, an essence characterised by freshness, abundance, and spontaneity. These values become enshrined in a 1960s 'still-life' layout, the orchestration of staged imageries, vivid colours redolent of market freshness, the now fashionable "Mediterranean diet", and hinting at the familiar hues of the Italian flag.

PROFESSOR IAIN MACRURY
Branded Content And Long-Form Semiotics:
The Case Of Snackmasters

60-years on, these motifs continue to inform many promotional communications for Pizza and Pasta (Sassatelli 2019; Ardizoni 2005).

Thus, the Panzani brand becomes the locus for a feeling of "Italian-icity" (Barthes 1977:33; Giardelli 2004). Pasta becomes *mythologised*[3]. Through a rhetorical-semiotic process enacted on the page of the magazine advertisement, a dry, bland, mechanically produced product becomes more digestible - refreshed - for the imagination and, so, also, for the busy shopper.

This process is obvious (and inevitable) - even if not acknowledged - we can all 'read' ads. But there are benefits in the work of teasing out or unravelling the text; work which semiotic conceptions and terminologies such as "denotation" and "connotation" can help us to do. Semiotics remains relevant today because its ethos and technical languages afford perspectives supporting critical and professional reflection on (promotional) sign formation, including in branded content. Semiotics, in this sense, becomes another means toward attentive critical and professional reflexivity.

Snackmasters: "gameshow-documentary branded content."

Now, fast forward to *Snackmasters*. Here we have a long-form narrative - not just a still life closed text ad but an extended 30-minute entertainment piece. Its lead presenter, TV personality Fred Sirieix sets out the show's stall. Each week a famous high street snack takes centre stage - in our case, Domino's Pizza. Sirieix proposes

> ....snacks like [Domino's] deserve the admiration and respect of fine dining connoisseurs. They're produced in their millions inside cutting-edge factories, and they taste perfect every time. (Snackmasters 2020)

He continues, setting up the challenge to the show's participants and the Channel 4 TV audience.

> But no one appreciates the genius of how they're made. So, each episode, I'm setting an extraordinary challenge. Two of the country's fanciest chefs will attempt to create exact replicas of famous snacks in their own kitchens. (Snackmasters 2020)

---

3 Barthes wrote an equally famous collection of essays called Mythologies (1957/2012) in which he used semiotics to explore the constructed signification of everyday signs – in an early and hugely influential example of popular semiotics applied to the everyday. Derived from this is the somewhat familiar language of the "brand myth" (see e.g. Luedickie et al 2010)

PROFESSOR IAIN MACRURY
Branded Content And Long-Form Semiotics: The Case Of Snackmasters

The scene is set for a light-hearted documentary exploration of Pizza (informing) and a fun duel between chefs.

Hybrid genres: documentary and game show - light 'factual' TV

Snackmasters offers a hybrid offspring of two genres, the game show, and the factory process documentary (Skivirsky 2020). First: The reality TV game format has become ubiquitous and needs no explaining. Shows such as *MasterChef* and *The Great British Bake-Off* offer relevant food-centric exemplars. Cooks compete in dramatised challenges and submit to the authoritative judgements of expert critics and legendary chefs. Audiences witness a ritual that affirms the cooks' merits and the judges' authority - the winner receives acknowledgement and repute. So, *Snakmasters* pits two top chefs against each other to recreate the iconic snack.

In addition, *Snackmasters* overlays a second ingredient genre — the industrial process documentary. Emerging from a long tradition in filmmaking stretching back to include, e.g. *A Visit to Peek Frean and Co.'s Biscuit Works* (1906), the 'industrial' (Abel 2004; Russell 2011), as the form came to be called, is familiar from decades of screen watching.

> *These were the films whose cameramen took their equipment past factory gates, to shoot in their interiors, summoning the magic of their medium to compress manufacturing, refining or assembly processes, usually hidden from public view, into mere minutes. (Russell 2011)*

The 'disclosure' of behind-the-scenes manufacture feeds on a popular fascination, including a celebration of industrial production. The genre promises a certain candour in that films disclose a usually 'hidden' process.

However, at the same time, the "insider" view typically offers a performative promotional tone, as the camera tends to marvel at the slickness of machinic processes - not to mention the evident skill of deft factory workers. Such 'backstage' disclosure of brands' manufacturing processes - often mesmeric in detail - adds authority and seems to offset anxious suspicions in consumers' minds, "I don't know where it comes from", and standard reservations associated with mass manufacture. "Oh, that looks good, amazing, better than I thought", etc., replace emergent doubts.

PROFESSOR IAIN MACRURY
Branded Content And Long-Form Semiotics:
The Case Of Snackmasters

These "industrials" (Russell 2011; Vernallis et al 2013) offered a peculiar sense of provenance - a (staged) reassurance highlighting machinic ingenuity over mere mechanical reproduction. The *Snackmasters* format is an inheritor of this filmic rhetoric - and the authority it lends to brands that deploy it. Each episode includes light touch invitations into the 'heart' of the brand in the style of 'industrials'

Recreating a Brand Icon from the inside out

The signature trope - chefs remaking the iconic foods - takes us further inside the object, whether Domino's, Quality Street, or KitKat. The format adds the lustre of Michelin-starred expertise and jaunty, "cheffy" creativity to the production mix. As with the Panzani ad, we've seen several ideas, concepts, and values brought together to stabilise and substantiate some mythologies about a brand, in this case, Domino's Pizza. Of course, Domino's is a well-known global brand. Its heritage includes a long association with American fast food. However, it retains a hint of its connection to the Italian origins of Pizza within its name Domino's, chosen explicitly for its resonance with the linguistic sound of Italian tongue[4] (Turner 2020:34) - echoes here of Barthes's (1977) "Panzani".

We are alert to the idea of Domino's as quick-delivery fare and, therefore, to the threat of its brand becoming associated with commodified mass processed low-value and unhealthy highly processed super-fast food. Such associations are risky for any brand and have become out of kilter within some influential strands of contemporary food discourse. Domino's is thriving, based explicitly on its offer of rapid, convenient delivery, available now through mobile devices at the touch of a button. It seems to be food without effort, and with the implication, food without craft, food which is at risk of seeming not just convenient but "throwaway" (cheap, bulk, "commodified" (Pine and Gilmore 1999). Especially as the Domino's product is not, in fact, that cheap, the brand must manage tensions in its meaning - navigating between associations of high-process and high-quality with great care.

The antitype of Domino's is artisanal, or elite pizza. Domino's is competing not just with other Pizza delivery companies, not just with fast food providers, but also with the idea of organic artisanal luxury slow, authentic, cooked, created, delicious, bespoke food – in or out of the home.

---

4 Turner 2020 reports an early brand decision:" "One day an employee came back from delivering a pizza and said, "I've got our name! Domino's!" I said, "That's great!" I'd never heard of a Domino's pizza before. It was Italian, and we could use a domino logo." (Turner 2020:34)

PROFESSOR IAIN MACRURY
Branded Content And Long-Form Semiotics: The Case Of Snackmasters

The traditional Italian restaurant scene shadows 'fast' Pizza consumption on one side, the quick, cheaper, ready-baked supermarket Pizza on the other. Domino's must stake a claim - to remain a meaningful choice - a compelling symbol for a complex (if banal) compromise formation binding in-home and out-of-home eating to our shifting lifestyles and desires.

The recent failure of the Domino's franchise in one notable territory provides an illustrative counterpoint. Domino's globally successful formal could not gain commercial (or semiotic) traction in Italy (the Pizza-motherland), closing 29 branches (Giuffrida 2022). Localities ingest (or reject) global brands in distinct ways.

Domino's brand faces a permanent task everywhere to celebrate its core values; convenience, quickness, red, white and blue American-global branding but offsetting the disbenefits in associations of mass manufacture and systemic, 'non-place' (Auge 1995), high-process production and delivery. In addition, the brand must re-incorporate something (just enough) of its connection to the craft heritage of Pizza - Italian-ness is a small but significant part of the jigsaw.

The *Snackmaster* format applied to Domino's offers an ingenious dramatisation of notable semiotic oppositions and tensions within the Dominos brands mythology. Semiotics' technical language became used to talk of binary oppositions (male-female, sun-moon, inside-outside, sacred-profane etc.) within the structure of a narrative or cultural myth. Similarly, we might see the Domino's brand myth playing with its core conflicts: fast/slow, sacred/profane, Italian/global, convenience/treat etc.

The *Snakmasters* Domino's episode follows two strands of brand-building exposition. First, heritage, a potted history of the brand, presents Domino's origins with American airmen returning to the US Post War - hankering after the recently enjoyed Pizza they had experienced in Italy in the 1940s. So, America and Italy are already in the DNA of the brand. Second, the growth of the now global brand and Domino's association with speedy delivery come to the fore.

Second, product and production, the Domino's Pizza becomes the mythic good object. A hyperbolic introduction sets a framework within which the subtle brand building plays out. Arriving at the Domino's fast food stop on a London High Street, we hear, you're in a place of worship, a fast food temple, a sacred place...Domino's Pizza, the largest Pizza company on planet Earth (*Snackmasters* 2020)

PROFESSOR IAIN MACRURY
Branded Content And Long-Form Semiotics: The Case Of Snackmasters

This strand of the episode includes what we might call the denotative level, a precise and straightforward process narrative that shows aspects of the manufacturing process - the Pizza-as-thing. A hands-on tutorial from a company operative amplifies this element of the story. She demonstrates the exact techniques, steps and timings of the Domino's Pizza manufacturing process. Further presentations complete the Pizza's journey - from the factory to delivery and from the Domino's kitchen to the customer.

Pizza identities politics: To be or not to be Italian

The additional primary ingredient in the genre mix is that the chefs are in 'banter-fuelled' competition with each other. The competition between the chefs in this mash-up adopts the guise of a game show or reality TV. In the *Bake-Off* style cooking competition, the protagonists receive careful introductions to identify their approachable ordinariness and hard-working success. Alongside this, the chefs' elite status, including recognition as Michelin-starred successful restauranteurs in select London locations.

Their authority as connoisseurs and creators is assured. The episode makes much play in framing the rivalry between a UK-based English chef versus a UK-based Italian chef. There is some tension as the Italian chef, permanently throughout the show, reiterates the potential humiliation arising from any failure in a competition. How can he fail in making some version of his national dish? On the opposing side, the spirited and hyper-ambitious English chef goes to every length to win the day.

The Italian has a lifelong history of Pizza making—heavy connotations of sporting rivalry highlight the encoded nationalities as the competition unfolds. The entertainment content of the programme in this narrative focuses on the rigorous efforts made by the chefs to replicate the Domino's recipe and successfully cook a pizza that might convince somebody that it was the real authentic Domino's Pizza.

Reversals and oppositions/copies and originals

Notice here then the reversal underscored in the structure of the 'plot'. The audience watches the chefs copying Domino's rather than Domino's portrayed, as a mass-produced 'fast-food' image of a pizza, a copy of the "real" thing. So, the narrative structure already provides a subtle confusion between authentic and inauthentic.

PROFESSOR IAIN MACRURY
Branded Content And Long-Form Semiotics: The Case Of Snackmasters

Snackmaster's format (re-)codes Domino's Pizza as the authentic culinary object within the semiotically marked bounds of the show's competition.

A second related reversal sees chefs not as masters but as students seeking to learn the proprietary skills of the Domino's brand. This scene includes the performative demo highlighting Domino's staff's mastery of making the classic Pepperoni Pizza. This tutorial is delivered to the Michelin-starred chefs, reduced to students as they take on their task of replicating the Domino's Pizza formula. They have nothing but their elite skills of being chefs. Nevertheless, there is entertainment to be had in watching the chefs make different iterations of their recipe copy and seeing their failures and successes in emulating Domino's original.

The culmination of the competitive narrative brings the chefs into a head-to-head cook-off. Under time pressure, they must produce their final effort to reproduce a Domino's Pizza - each time, the chef's "copy" is compared directly to a 'real' Domino's product.

Judgment, authority and authentication

Judgement forms the final highly significant moment. The denouement of the competition narrative situates the chefs facing three senior Domino's staff, a regional business partner, an Operations Director and a Product Manager. The executives taste the efforts, adopting the knowingness of connoisseurs, alongside a tone reminiscent of commercial quality control.

The show format positions the brand executives, and so Domino's, as authoritative arbiters, deciding between the chef's efforts and conferring evaluative judgement. Domino's managers are (now) the masters of culinary quality. So, in the semiotic universe of the show, tables are turned. The sacred chefs defer to the profane commercial high street brand. They await the judgments of the corporate managers of Domino's Pizza, rather than, as we might expect, them passing their judgement on the everyday fare. The show cleverly integrates competing forms of authority within the more comprehensive Dominos myth. This is a dramatic, if subtle semiotic transformation.

The final decision shows that the Italian chef has just edged it. His dough has been left maturing for a more extended period and has a bit more flavour.

PROFESSOR IAIN MACRURY
Branded Content And Long-Form Semiotics:
The Case Of Snackmasters

The outcome secures the 'slow' element of a fast-food pizza re-encoding craft in the brand palette, and the Italian chef, on-screen at least, comes into the Domino's fold. So, we find in the combination of two narratives (the process narrative and the competition narrative) that Domino's Pizza and its brand become re-validated as a worthy standard, an object of aspiration even for the best chefs, including even the best Italian chefs. In their struggles, the chefs acknowledge the quickness, efficiency, consistency and presentation characteristic of fast food. Essentially the values of McDonaldization (Ritzer) remain reaffirmed and intact in the brand palette. The episode subtly re-invests Italianicity back into the meaning of the brand, alongside a reaffirmed sense of the quality, efficiency and rigour of the Domino's process.

Snackmasters constitutes essentially, then, a 30-minute advertisement for the Domino's brand. The balance of sacred and profane in the semiotic cosmology of Pizza has been nudged, if ever so slightly, in favour of the idea of Domino's as 'the real thing' (Eco 2014). The brand edges into our mind as a more authentic premium pizza choice. We may feel drawn into the feeling of being 'schooled' in the Domino's myth.

Indeed, combined with the somewhat comedic light entertainment reality show idiom – *Snackmasters* open-hearted brand voice can become quite compelling, whichever product is centre stage. As we watch, it is difficult to tell the extent to which the brand is the subject of the show - its speaker or author? Or, conversely, if it is the object of the show (as in a light-hearted documentary), so an object for exposure, ridicule, or critique. But whatever the answer, for 30-minutes, the week's brand plays vividly in the audience's mind. A quick look at Twitter while the Domino's episode was broadcast confirms its promotional effect - threads of viewers drooling over the prospect of a hot Pizza - or the myth of one! Branded entertainment at work.

References

Abel, R. (2004). Encyclopedia of early cinema: Routledge.

Ardizzoni, M. (2005). Mediating Italianess: Television, identity, and globalization. Indiana University.

Augé, M. (1995). Non-places: Introduction to an Anthropology of Supermodernity: verso.

Barthes, R. (1977). Image-music-text: Macmillan.

Barthes, R. (2012). Mythologies: The complete edition. NY: Hill and Wang.

Danesi, M. (2017). Visual rhetoric and semiotic. In Oxford research encyclopedia of communication.

Danesi, M. (2018). Of cigarettes, high heels, and other interesting things: An introduction to semiotics: Springer.

Eco, U. (2014). Faith in fakes: Random House.

Freans, P. (Writer). (1906). A Visit to Peek Frean and Co.'s Biscuit Works (1906) - extract. In.

Girardelli, D. (2004). Commodified identities: The myth of Italian food in the United States. Journal of Communication Inquiry, 28(4), 307-324.

Guiffrida, A. (10 August 2022). Domino's retreats from Italy having failed to conquer the home of pizza - The Guardian.

Lawes, R. (2002). Demystifying semiotics: some key questions answered. International Journal of Market Research, 44(3), 1-10.

Lawes, R. (2020). Using semiotics in marketing: How to achieve consumer insight for brand growth and profits: Kogan Page Publishers.

Levy, S. J. (1987). Semiotician ordinaire. Marketing and Semiotics, Mouton de Gruyter, Berlin, 13-20.

Lotman, M. (2002). Umwelt and semiosphere. Sign Systems Studies, 30(1), 33-39.

Lotman, Y. M. (1990). Universe of the Mind. A semiotic theory of culture, 20-35.

Lotman, Y. M. (1990). Universe of the Mind. A semiotic theory of culture, 20-35.

Luedicke, M. K., Thompson, C. J., & Giesler, M. (2010). Consumer identity work as moral protagonism: How myth and ideology animate a brand-mediated moral conflict. Journal of Consumer Research, 36(6), 1016-1032.

Lury, C., & Warde, A. (1997). Investments in the imaginary consumer. Buy this book: Studies in advertising and consumption, 87-102.

Nöth, W. (1988). The language of commodities Groundwork for a semiotics of consumer goods. International Journal of Research in Marketing, 4(3), 173-186.

Oswald, L. R., & Oswald, L. (2012). Marketing semiotics: Signs, strategies, and brand value: Oxford University Press.

Russell, P. (2011). From acorn to oak: industrial and corporate films in Britain. Business Archives, 103, 53-76.

Sassatelli, R. (2019). Introduction: Food, Foodways and Italianicity. In Italians and food (pp. 1-15): Springer.

Sassatelli, R. (2019). Italians and food: Springer.

Skvirsky, S. A. (2020). The Process Genre. In The Process Genre: Duke University Press.

Turner, M. L. (2020). The Domino's Story: How the Innovative Pizza Giant Used Technology to Deliver a Customer Experience Revolution: HarperCollins Leadership.

Vernallis, C., Herzog, A., & Richardson, J. (2013). The Oxford handbook of sound and image in digital media: Oxford University Press.

Williamson, J. (1978). Decoding advertisements (Vol. 4): Marion Boyars London.

Professor Iain MacRury is Professor in Communications, Media and Culture at the University of Stirling. Previous to this he was Deputy Dean, Research and Professional Practice in the Faculty of Media and Communication at Bournemouth University. Iain has researched and published widely on Brand Communications, Mobile Communications, the theory of comedy, science fiction, Olympic mega events, Paralympics, urban change and local development, higher education policy and practice. He has a special interest in psychosocial approaches to culture and communication.

SILVIA VELASCO PRAGA
Metaverse And The Future Of Branded Content

Over the years, branded content has evolved aligned with the changes in society and consumers, embracing new trends in their interests, habits and media consumption. Since Guide Michelin pioneered brands' efforts to trespass advertising and capture clients' attention beyond its products, it's been a century now! Magazines, TV promotions, movies, dolls, books, videogames... brands have tried and exploited all means and media to engage with their audience by providing relevant and useful information, entertainment or experiences.

Until a decade ago branded content was mainly unidirectional: the brand provided something interesting to the audience, expecting to get -directly or indirectly- sales and ROI in return. Since digital became mass media and social networks exploded, brands need first to listen to the audience, provide usefulness, be consistent across all touchpoints and, finally, interact and respond to the consumers. Communication between brands and audiences is now bidirectional. This new paradigm has complicated and sophisticated how branded content and content marketing need to be conceptualized and delivered but it has also expanded the scope and opportunities for the brands. Ironically, there are more media and communication windows than ever but consumer attention has become evasive and tricky.

In the past months, everything seems to happen in the metaverse. Metaverse is the new 'New'. Despite the facts that there are still serious technological barriers and that there is NO significant volume of audience in the metaverse(s), brands are tempted to explore and exploit this new promised land.

Nevertheless, it is true: the incipient metaverse, extended reality and their alike will transcend all the barriers we have known and will make human communication profoundly evolve and then, will transform marketing and advertising. This new virtual universe will expand our digital life to an unlimited number of virtual worlds and to communities of millions of digital human beings. We just need to observe how a child interacts in Roblox or Minecraft in order to understand that it is not a videogame: our identity will transcend physical barriers and it will be us experiencing and driving the game.

SILVIA VELASCO PRAGA
Metaverse And The Future Of Branded Content

So, the foundation of metaverse is already here and it is immersive, three-dimensional, collaborative, non-stop and unlimited.

For brands, it means a multidirectional landscape where they will not only interact with the consumers, but they will need to collaborate and co-create with them. For branded content, the implications are many and quite straight-forward. Brands will need to offer an attractive, differential and coherent full experience across all these digital worlds and lives. Otherwise, brands will go unnoticed or they might even generate rejection.

Brands will also need to re-think branded content projects or, at least, those tactical branded content initiatives that are popping up everywhere today. In this new paradigm, brands' communications cannot be limited to a campaign or a specific moment because (the) metaverse and their allies break the traditional narrative arc and a non-stop presence of the brands will be required. And brands will need to be authentic, active and useful elements of the metaverse.

Probably the concept 'brand content' will fall short in the future and will be replaced by 'brand-verse experience' or some new cool concept, which will integrate - at least in 'part-phygital' touchpoints, content, advertising and products. When? From my humble point of view, there is no point in asking ourselves this question just to know how much we should or can wait. Mobile phones or social networks did not explode from one day to the next but they became massive and indispensable in a very short time. . consumers have always been the early adopters who have brought and guided brands into new territories. Metaverse is a nice playground to explore and to experiment. Although brands need to calibrate immediate expectations, the moment is now.

Silvia Velasco Praga is the CEO of BE A LION (Mediaset Group) and VP Innovation and Development at BCMA Spain. As CEO of BE A LION (formerly known as Animal M), Silvia brings a deep knowledge of the development of Branded Content in the digital field, as developers of projects such as El Gran Reto Solidario and Samsung MadFun. In addition, Silvia has extensive experience working in multinationals such as Google and at print and radio media.

OLGIERD CYGAN
The Real Branded Content

Do you know when for the first time, I seriously thought about branded content?

It was back in 2001, whilst watching The Hire, a movie funded by BMW with an amazing line up of 'A-List' stars – in front of and behind the cameras.

Unlike the other productions, where product placement was generally the best we could see, this was the REAL branded content. The brand was 'front and centre' from the very beginning. But in the right way. Not as an added element at the end of the production process.

Now fast forward to 2022 and frankly, there are not so many other projects that are top of my mind.

OR at least, not so many, as I could dream off. Despite all the wisdom how of brands should engage with their customers, the number of great branded content projects is not that extensive – or as extensive as it should be.

While scouting for interesting projects to be presented during my Filmteractive Festival[1], I always have a challenge to find enough great branded content projects. OR maybe I should say ground-breaking.

Usually, 3 to 5 a year, but not 30 to 50 to choose from. Luckily with advancement of digital advertising and the rise of online video, not to mention the new wave of creators on platforms like Instagram, TikTok and YouTube, there are more and more engaging digital branded content projects each year.

But the real game changer is about to come - the Metaverse. Looking how quickly the brands are jumping on 'the new train', trying to secure their position in the upcoming transition from 'Web2' to 'Web3', I foresee a great time for branded content in years ahead.

---

1 https://filmteractive.eu

OLGIERD CYGAN
The Real Branded Content

Olgierd Cygan is CEO of Smart Engine and Managing Partner of Future.Company. He is also the Founder of Filmteractive Festival. A digital enthusiast, entrepreneur and educator with over 20 years of experience. Ex-Deloitte partner, Olgierd's digital adventure started in 1995 in one of the first digital agencies in Poland. In 1999, shortly after graduation, he founded his own agency – Digital One. In 2004-2009, the agency was responsible for digital offering within the Euro RSCG Group in Poland (now Havas). From 2009, Digital One focused on a strategic approach to digital. That led to the next game changing decision. In 2015, D1 was acquired by Deloitte, and Deloitte Digital CE was formed based on his company. For 3 years, he's been actively involved in building the new type of creative digital consultancy. He has learned valuable lessons of international collaboration and digital transformation methods. He has now returned to the entrepreneurial role in 2019 – building a 'next gen' digital professional services group of companies around Welcome Digital and Hello Consulting. Olgierd is President of BCMA Poland and a member of the BCMA Global Council.

MARIANA LORENA
Brand Content: Effectively Effective. How To?

Brand Content is no longer a 'nice to have' but a 'must have' in any brand's communication strategy. No matter what line of business a brand belongs to, traditional advertising, by itself, is no longer enough to connect and truly engage consumers.

As media consumption becomes less linear and more digital, consumers gain endless power over who, what, when and where they choose to engage with, and brands need to make an extra effort to stay relevant.

In this context, Brand Content has shown up as an excellent tool to help brands build and keep relevancy.

However, it is most important, and not always easy to find the right strategy, the right formula, the right format to engage a target audience. And not all Brand Content is effectively effective.

In fact, producing quality Brand Content takes time and thought.

It requires market and consumer research and insight to identify the most relevant passion points, e.g. music, cinema, fashion, environment, cause-led, sports, etc. Sometimes it might have nothing to do with the brand's product or service itself only with what is relevant to the audience that you wish to engage with.

It requires creativity to tell the best story, with the right characters, in the right tone, through the right perspective.

It requires strategic thinking and planning to leverage reach and impact whether on air (e.g. TV and Radio), online (e.g. Video or Social Media) or even on the ground (e.g. any type of event).

Is requires consistency because it should be an ongoing communication platform. Once a brand onboards a Brand Content strategy it should keep it 'nourished' as well as other marketing disciplines. This is the best way to achieve outstanding results.

MARIANA LORENA
Brand Content: Effectively Effective. How To?

And above all it requires authenticity. It is useless for a brand to claim a "content territory" when it's values and actions are not aligned with that territory.

Building a long-lasting Brand Content strategy is all about exposing a brand's identity and beliefs and transforming that into something that either entertains or is useful to consumers. This immediate trade-off is essential for the success of the content produced. If it does not fulfil at least one of these needs, then even with a high level of media investment on top the probability of success is very limited. On the other hand, if the brand content easily entertains, teaches and/or informs then even organically it will have the power to disseminate.

And what about measurement? No, you can't. You can't just expect to measure a Brand Content strategy just like you measure a TV or Digital Campaign. Sure, some of these metrics can be used but depending on the goal and the format other KPIs should be taken into consideration and evaluated in the long-term.

A brand's commitment to a successful Brand Content strategy is something to be looked upon in the long-term from the initial phase that identifies the opportunity, decides the strategy and the creativity to the final phase when results are delivered and achieved. If it becomes a long-lasting relationship, then it will be 'effectively effective'.

Mariana Lorena is a Director at FUSE Portugal, Omnicom Media Group's content, experience and activation agency. She is an experienced professional, responsible for the leadership, management of content and brand activation. Mariana develops creative and strategic content proposals including brand experiences, digital solutions, influencer marketing and profile management.

ARMANDO DÍAZ
The Mind & Heart for Everlasting Content

Recently in our agency, we were debating whether to include a case study in a presentation because it had been launched more than 7-years ago. "Is it still relevant? It's been several years..." We concluded that the answer was yes, it was still as relevant as it will ever be, and it will continue to be relevant in the coming years.

The conundrum got me thinking about how a great content strategy, built from the mind and heart, never expires.

The case study was for a major US airline that, every day, flies thousands of travellers between the United States and our home region, the Caribbean. The Caribbean is an amazing melting pot of cultures, adventures, and destinations but over the last 60 years, the diasporas have had a big impact on the population.

A diverse and highly skilled demographic leaving their homes in search of opportunities in another country is not exclusive to the region, but it hits straight home. Puerto Rico is one of the countries in the region impacted by this behaviour since before the 2000s, and there are now more Puerto Ricans living abroad than on the Island.

Puerto Ricans are emotionally attached to their loved ones, especially to their grandparents. Our team's research led us to key insights based on 1) separation and 2) connection.

Families living in different countries would constantly look for ways to stay in contact and maintain that special bond between grandparents and grandkids. The separation would be mostly for economic reasons. In some cases, years would pass before they met in person again. The airline was presented with an opportunity to amplify a relevant human situation, which leads me to the 1st part of great content:

> **The Mind** - the essential captain that guides our wonderful journey and the key to navigating a brand through a successful strategy. The foundation for any strategy is research and discovery. Over 86 billion neurons fire to connect information and find that much-needed insight for the next step.

ARMANDO DÍAZ
The Mind & Heart for Everlasting Content

After establishing that insight, the creative and communications team at the agency, alongside the airline, worked on an idea to surprise a selected group of families by reuniting kids with their grandparents and film the emotional moment. The diaspora was cut short for just a moment in time. The airline secretly flew the grandkids to meet with their grandparents while psychologists and brand experts gave a lecture about family, the diaspora, and the values of the company. After the lecture, the kids came out to greet their grandparents. It was a beautiful surprise for everyone! The moment was filled with smiles, tears, hugs, kisses, and gratitude.

The story was picked up by all the main local media news outlets, increased the positive brand sentiment, won several awards, and was even talked about during a church sermon by a priest ("They seized the opportunity...it touches everyone...that is professional creativity..."). This leads me to the 2nd part of great content:

> **The Heart** – the finely-skilled master that beats 100,000 times a day. It orchestrates our essence and is always referenced symbolically as our emotional motor; this is to whom a brand must tell a story. Strategies must be humanized, developed as a simple narrative, and connect to any person that is paying attention.

I've watched the case study video over 50 times and, almost 8-years later, it still brings me to tears. The connection remains as pure and relevant as it was on the first day. It's not for the faint of heart!

The strategy for most brands focuses on what they are selling instead of shifting to a more inward-thinking narrative that transforms into a bigger purpose. It's like trying to convince someone to purchase a home without visiting the living room or befriend someone without speaking to them. Brands should be brave enough to embrace vulnerability and create everlasting content strategies that will continue to connect throughout a lifetime. The mind and heart last a lifetime...shouldn't great content do the same too?

Armando Díaz is the Community Engagement Manager at Lopito, Ileana & Howie, one of Puerto Rico's leading creative agencies. He is a bilingual Digital Marketer & Strategist with experience developing multichannel brand campaigns and data driven strategies for a diverse portfolio of clients. Armando is a firm believer in brand growth through community-building strategies, in Design Thinking and how data can transform businesses.

CHANTAL RICKARDS OBE
Think Different

Fellow creatives who have been making branded content for as long as I can remember have not been getting the credit they deserve.

As a producer for 30 years of traditional TV shows for ITV, BBC, Sky, UKTV and Channel 4 (*Through the Keyhole, This Morning, Countdown, MasterChef* etc.) as well as shows funded by brands for Channel 4, ITV, Channel 5 and BBC World News (*Specsavers' TV Book Club, Morrisons' Farm Camp, Spar's Meals in Moments* and *Citibank's One Day In*), I can honestly say there is little difference in terms of the creativity that was brought to bear and the diligence and hard work that went into making them. Were editorial principles blunted?

Not by a long way! If anything, the extra layer of scrupulous overseers made me more careful about the stories I crafted and the way I told them. But there were other benefits too.

As regulators push back and advertisers push forward, we still seem to be in a place where these two worlds of equally valid content creators are still at odds with each other, if only in the eyes of those in the business. In the main, viewers, users and consumers barely notice the difference, and that's the point: the messaging should be so subtle as to not hit them over the back of the head with a mallet, more that it should allow them to feel warm towards the brand and let their sentiment run riot when they get to the shopping aisles. People really don't care who has paid for it and they don't feel jaundiced by it either.

Just before lockdown I came back from Los Angeles – where I'd been for five-years – having left WPP media agency MEC for the heady heights of Hollywood to run BAFTA over there. Content there is undoubtably king, where a whole city of people has come together to create the world's best stories, many of whom are Brits. What I noticed was that there is a much greater appreciation for the whole content ecosystem which allows brands to have a much greater share-of-voice and an equally posh director's chair at the table. Brands work 'symbiotically' with studios and the like, not 'parasitically' as some might expect; they are after all financially supporting the whole industry with advertising in cinemas, on TV and through online and social media businesses.

CHANTAL RICKARDS OBE
Think Different

In the USA producers, movie theatres, directors, studios, talent, networks, and distributors have much greater respect for what brands can bring to the party, and not just money. Brands also can attract audiences to big ideas and clever concepts and to bring a level of sophistication and research to content makers that is enviable, even to the biggest players in the market.

They can also work directly with talent – and keeping talent happy is an art form in its own right – so what's not to like? Who better understands the world of children than toy manufacturers and confectioners? Who better understands the world of Gen-Z than apparel brands and booze companies?

I have witnessed these same professionals gathering round a table with content makers and sharing information about what makes consumers (audiences!) tick, what they like and why, where their aspirations lie and how they want to live their lives – so why wouldn't you heartily invite them to the party?

For anyone still unsure if they should allow brands to get embedded with content, all I would say is, give them a voice at the table and the respect they deserve and to *Just Do It!*

Chantal Rickards OBE is a Film and TV Executive, Former CEO of BAFTA Los Angeles and Head of Programming and Branded Content at MEC (now Wavemaker). She has extensive expertise in content production, international media, advertising and the arts. An accomplished international public speaker, she has the understanding and ability to facilitate, coach and mentor others. She is passionate about collaborating with organisations to grow the value of the business and effect impactful change.

GREG TURZYNSKI
It's Time To Get Noticed

You've made some content and distributed it across a range of digital channels (digital accounts for 75% of Advertising spend[1]).

You report a huge number of impressions. A video impression requires 2 continuous seconds of play[2].

You quote an engagement rate based on likes, shares, comments etc. Industry average engagement rate is 0.064%[3]. So, 99.36% did nothing.

You probably wonder if it had any effect. Advertising on Facebook and YouTube faded from memory quickly and had an impact on sales for little more than six days, whereas TV advertising's impact on sales lasted 10 times longer[4].

You delivered the required impressions at a discount of 10% compared with the previous campaign. However, only 51% of what you've spent made it to the Media Owner and 15% vanished[5]!

So, did you get noticed?

All the above are averages and of course some advertisers will do far better. However, if these are averages, those below the average need to have a serious think about their approach.

If you think about the digital display channels you are using, particularly the social channels that take the majority of your expenditure, what were they built on and what is their most popular content?

The answer is talented people. People who get noticed, a lot! So, why not use the very thing that made digital so successful.

---

1 Advertising Association 2023 forecast in October 2022
2 According to The Media Rating Council / IAB, to qualify for counting as a viewable video ad impression, it is required that 2 continuous seconds of the video advertisement is played
3 The 2021 median average engagement rate per post (by follower) on Facebook is 0.064%, across all industries
4 ThinkTV 2018
5 51% of your Programmatic spend reaches the Media Owner and 15% simply vanishes – Programmatic Supply Chain Transparency Study PWC / ISBA October 2020

GREG TURZYNSKI
It's Time To Get Noticed

Nike is a big brand with 38 million Followers on Facebook. They sponsor Ronaldo, who has four times more Followers – 156 million! (Dec 2022).

But where do you start?

The first thing to understand is that there are two distinct elements. Firstly, it is the creativity of the talent. They built their following and you need them involved to ensure an authentic and effective outcome. Secondly, it is ultimately their fans that you are going to be reaching; they are your target audience.

To date, it is unclear how Brands choose Talent. We can see what they are noticed for, but we know little about their fans other than rather inaccurate and duplicated head counts on social platforms.

This needed to change and so, The One Partnership has invested heavily in a new approach to Talent and Brands.

They have now applied genuine rigour to this issue by integrating their own first party data with market leading syndicated tools to truly understand the relationship between talent fans and consumers. This uncovers actionable insights to develop more effective communications. This is unique.

Awareness of Piers Morgan sits at a whopping 98.76%. No big surprise that 45% of people in the UK think negatively about Piers Morgan and also, no big surprise that 30% think positively. A brand partnership with Marmite is perhaps quite relevant.

In addition, it is possible to identify the Brands that fans use and at what frequency. We can also identify their demographic and geographic makeup and media usage. We can also look at their attitudes and values to identify target audiences based on the most complex Brand communications objectives.

In a simple example overleaf, regular users of Greggs index extremely highly with fans of Piers Morgan. That is because he's been very vocal about Vegan Sausage Rolls. Perhaps there is no such thing as bad publicity! They are mostly Male, Gen X, living in Suburbs who are interested in Celebrity News / Gossip and can best be reached via Facebook.

GREG TURZYNSKI
It's Time To Get Noticed

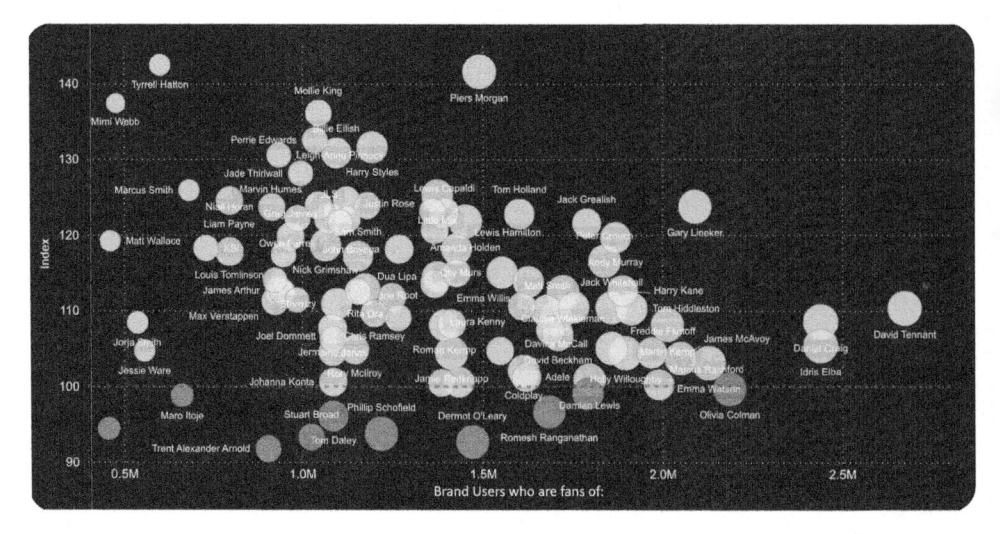

So, Talent becomes a Channel of communication with all the data necessary to justify, plan, authenticate and measure the outcome. They are media.

This approach has led to some great successes. You can watch Niall Horan's Homecoming with Lewis Capaldi on Amazon Prime developed by The One Partnership, Electric Robin and Guinness. This is Guinness' first Branded Content of this type.

The One Partnership's research 'FANATIQTM' profiled over 200 celebrities from the world of Music, Sport & Film against the brand and the target audience.

The profile analysis discovered significant key insights:

> 1. Musicians are the ultimate influencers for our target audience, indexing 84% above base
>
> 2. Music is where current GUINNESS advocates and the target audience coalesces
>
> 3. Genuine GUINNESS brand advocates Niall Horan and Lewis Capaldi sat in the top 10 of the 'popular music artists' for 'Fan engagement with brand endorsement'.

Additionally, it was possible to identify that despite a fragmented home TV market, cultural moments, especially when supported by an earned strategy featuring icons, would resonate. Branded entertainment works by building connections in our memory between enjoyable content and a brand - and transferring positive emotion from one to the other.

GREG TURZYNSKI
It's Time To Get Noticed

'Homecoming' captured the two globally recognised musicians on an incredible road trip, filmed over 3 days. A stunningly shot and emotive journey, the film showcased the best of modern, vibrant Ireland and allowed for an exploration of a variety of Guinness brand values – particularly camaraderie and friendship, in an authentic and engaging format.

The film was subtly branded throughout via location and natural placement, and never deviated from its primary aim to entertain above brand exposure. It was unscripted to allow the artists' passions, personalities, and relationship to take centre stage. This approach provided talent with creative freedom in each phase (concept ideation, filming and edit). A 'Talent first' approach is critical to authenticity but providing this level of creative control was a major challenge for the project. There were concerns around losing sight of the overall brand purpose objectives, as well as brand compliance. To mitigate this, we built a clear and digestible content framework for talent to work towards. An exceptionally close working relationship between brand and talent ensured issues were alleviated and the content remained relevant throughout.

A strong earned and phased amplification strategy drove considerable conversation with the target audience about Homecoming and Guinness. The mid-October prime Sunday evening slot on national TV generated maximum viewership and cultural impact across online and traditional media. This conversation was supported by bespoke and shareable content activated through the talent's owned channels. Global audiences, within strategically important markets, could and still can access the show on Amazon Prime.

Results: Homecoming generated huge Awareness, built Affinity, boosted consideration, and delivered significant Business growth. And the vast majority of those who watched it called for more – loudly.

It got noticed.

Greg Turzynski is CEO of Global Living Brands and Chief Strategy Officer at The One Partnership. Greg started his career at Y&R, where hie rose to Executive Media Director. He moved on to become Managing Director of ZenithOptimedia, the largest media buyer at the time. Greg was also part of the team that achieved Investors in People and launched 'The ROI Agency' proposition for ZenithOptimedia. Greg has served on the IPA Training and Development Committee and the IPA Client Service Committee. Greg is a Global Advisor to the BCMA.

GREG TURZYNSKI
It's Time To Get Noticed

Nike is a big brand with 38 million Followers on Facebook. They sponsor Ronaldo, who has four times more Followers – 156 million! (Dec 2022).

But where do you start?

The first thing to understand is that there are two distinct elements. Firstly, it is the creativity of the talent. They built their following and you need them involved to ensure an authentic and effective outcome. Secondly, it is ultimately their fans that you are going to be reaching; they are your target audience.

To date, it is unclear how Brands choose Talent. We can see what they are noticed for, but we know little about their fans other than rather inaccurate and duplicated head counts on social platforms.

This needed to change and so, The One Partnership has invested heavily in a new approach to Talent and Brands.

They have now applied genuine rigour to this issue by integrating their own first party data with market leading syndicated tools to truly understand the relationship between talent fans and consumers. This uncovers actionable insights to develop more effective communications. This is unique.

Awareness of Piers Morgan sits at a whopping 98.76%. No big surprise that 45% of people in the UK think negatively about Piers Morgan and also, no big surprise that 30% think positively. A brand partnership with Marmite is perhaps quite relevant.

Greg Turzynski is CEO of Global Living Brands and Chief Strategy Officer at The One Partnership. Greg started his advertising career at Young & Rubicam in London, where his roles included Broadcast Director and Executive Media Director. Running the COI's Centralised TV Buying involved, 11 Government Privatisations from British Gas (success) to British Petroleum (failure). During this period, UIP distributed 214 films including Top Gun, Licence To Kill and Forrest Gump to name a few. He moved on to become Managing Director of Optimedia and MD of the merged ZenithOptimedia, the largest media buyer at the time. Greg was also part of the team that achieved Investors in People for Optimedia and launched 'The ROI Agency' proposition for ZenithOptimedia. Greg has served on the IPA Training and Development Committee and the IPA Client Service Committee. Greg is a Global Advisor to the BCMA.

JO FARMER, GERAINT LLOYD-TAYLOR, ALAN HUNT & EMILY STIRLING
Influencing Your Relationship: Key Points For Brands To Consider When Contracting With An Influencer

Influencers provide brands with an exciting and engaging way to reach audiences. Unlike traditional advertising, when working with influencers brands usually won't have complete control over the content which is created.

This means that brands must have a considerable degree of trust in the influencer, and this usually runs both ways. The relationship between the brand and influencer therefore needs to be built on a solid foundation. In practical terms, that foundation is enshrined in the contract between the brand and influencer. These are the key areas you should bear in mind when documenting your relationship with an influencer. These topics are relevant whether a brand contracts directly with the influencer or indirectly, such as through an agency.

Compliance and disclosure

Compliance should be right at the top of your list! The laws and rules which govern advertising in the UK (which are mainly to be found in the CAP Codes and reflect consumer protection laws) are sophisticated and well-trodden – and they apply to influencer marketing. It is important that the contract makes clear to influencers that they must comply with all applicable laws, advertising regulations and the latest guidance – remember, the guidance is updated often! This means, among other things, that they must not make misleading claims about products and services.

Also, a recurring theme among regulators is that of transparency. The influencer must disclose that they have been paid to promote or mention a brand, product, or service, or that they have been given or loaned something by a brand which has led them to mention the brand, product, or service. The contract should make clear what kind of disclosure is required - usually #ad or Ad at the very start of their posts. It isn't possible for a brand to absolve itself of responsibility, or to push all the responsibility for compliance and disclosure onto the influence r but it is something the contract must be clear about from the outset.

Editorial Control

This can be a tricky area for a brand owner and influencer to negotiate as authenticity of voice is key to any influencer – and that's often one of the main reasons why brands want to work with them. Of course, there are also brand messages that any advertiser will want to ensure come across. Consider how much editorial control you need and what you are looking to achieve. If the promotion is intended to be authentic to ensure maximum reach with the influencer's audience, you may opt for less control (except to ensure the relevant disclosure is used), but if you operate in a more regulated sector you may wish to have more control over the final messaging. Clearly setting out the nature and extent of the editorial control in the contract will avoid any surprises. An editorial control clause can, for example, insist that all materials created by the influencer rare submitted to you for prior approval, and allow for several reasonable amendments to be requested by the advertiser, as well as setting out a minimum number of posts, the timing of posts, claims/hashtags to be included, and so on.

Quality of audience

The right audience is required to help you deliver that return on investment. That's why you have picked a particular influencer. But what about the quality of that audience? Unfortunately, the rise of fake likes and bots continues but it's important to recognise that, particularly if the influencer's fee is directly related to the number of results, click throughs, likes, etc. Consider including a clause that prohibits the influencer from engaging in any practices which artificially increase the perceived engagement with the content and entitles you to terminate the contract if this does happen.

Exclusivity

You've found the perfect influencer they are on-brand, share your values and you know that they will resonate well with the audience you want to reach. Unfortunately, this means that they will probably also resonate well with the audiences your competitors want to reach! There is a simple fix to this – negotiating some form of exclusivity to ensure that the influencer does not also promote the brands, products, and services of your competitors for a pre-agreed period (usually during the term of the campaign and for a short period afterwards). Depending on the commercial circumstances of the arrangement, this is not an unreasonable ask, but it is always about striking the right balance.

Appearances and other obligations

Beyond posts, if you want the influencer to make any personal appearances, attend shoot days or perform any other services as part of the arrangement, these should be clearly set out in the contract, including what is expected of the influencer as part of each obligation, e.g., arriving on time, complying with reasonable directions of the venue or on set, being appropriately dressed (not wearing branded clothing unless asked to do so), etc. You should also consider if any specific insurance is needed, and, if so, require the influencer to co-operate with you and your insurer in the securing of that insurance and to comply with its requirements.

Usage period

While it is critical to decide how long an influencer's initial support will be required (often known as the "Campaign Period"), you should also consider building in the option to extend this period if the campaign is going well. An extension which is only discussed later in the relationship would normally require agreement between both parties, but if agreed at the outset, the contract could include an automatic right for you to extend the period in which you can continue to associate the brand with the influencer and/or require the influencer to continue to promote the brand for a reasonable, pre-agreed fee.

Warranties and undertakings

The importance of legal promises Don't be put off by the wording. 'Warranties' are simply assurances about things which have already happened or about the current situation when the contract is entered into. For example, the influencer should warrant that they do not have a criminal record (important for most brands), the influencer has not worked with any of your competitors in the (recent) past, and the influencer is in a fit and healthy state and able to be involved in the campaign. Some warranties will be relevant only in particular circumstances, e.g., that the influencer has a full, clean, valid UK driving licence if they will be required to promote a car brand.

When negotiating which warranties to include, you can flush out any past behaviours or issues you need to know about. 'Undertakings' are like warranties, but rather than providing assurances about the past or present they look to the future, including throughout the period of the contract.

JO FARMER, GERAINT LLOYD-TAYLOR, ALAN HUNT & EMILY STIRLING
Influencing Your Relationship: Key Points For Brands To Consider When Contracting With An Influencer

For example, the influencer should undertake that they will not say anything disparaging about your brand, that they will not bring themselves or the brand into disrepute (e.g., by saying racist, sexist, xenophobic things), and so on.

Termination

We know it's hard to envisage the end of your relationship before it has even started – but it's important that you do. A right to exit the relationship with any influencer is fundamental, not only because marketing budgets and direction can change suddenly but also because brand safety will be key for any brand. Your agreement with the influencer should specify certain rights for you to end your relationship early if necessary. This might be because of a breach by the influencer of their warranties or undertakings, or any obligations (e.g., failure to appear or failure to use the necessary disclosures in a post), or simply because you need to bring the campaign to an end. There is no one-size-fits-all here so give careful thought to whether, why and how you might want to end your relationship with an influencer, and what you will expect from them at that point.

Jo Farmer is a Partner at Lewis Silkin, and jointly leads the firm's Digital, Commerce & Creative group and advises clients on their advertising and marketing campaigns and exploitation of intellectual property rights and content.

Geraint Lloyd-Taylor is a Partner at Lewis Silkin, in the firm's Advertising & Marketing team. He advises numerous well known ad agencies, and some of the biggest brands in the world, in relation to their advertising campaigns and sales promotions.

Alan Hunt is a Partner at Lewis Silkin, in the Digital, Commerce & Creative team specialising in the drafting and negotiation of commercial and technology contracts and the development, protection and exploitation of intellectual property assets.

Emily Stirling is an Associate at Lewis Silkin, in the Commercial team. She completed her undergraduate degree in Law at the University of Birmingham, after which she moved in to the legal industry, initially in an HR role and then as a governance advisor, working with senior management to set the strategic agenda for a multinational law firm.

NINA GLYNN
Ad Blockers, Advertainment, And Advocacy: Why Gen-Z Is Blocking Paid Ads In Favour Of Real Voices

How to beat the ad blockers and connect with youth audiences via authentic brand advocacy. Armed with ad blockers, volume control and the almighty skip button, consumers are pulling out all the stops to resist traditional advertising. With the finger of 99% of customers poised and ready to hit skip, and 63% of consumers' browsers bulwarked with ad blockers, advertising is undergoing a reckoning.

From billboards and posters to streaming ads and pop-ups, advertising's metamorphosis has only increased consumer frustration. As it becomes more advanced, it becomes more intrusive - and consumers are refusing to play along.

But when every door closes, another opens. From the troubles of traditional advertising grew influencer marketing, and from the complaints of inauthenticity in influencer marketing grew genuine customer advocacy. Tracking the transition from advertising to advertainment to advocacy brings us to the most authentic and effective solution of all. Welcome to a new dawn of marketing, where symmetrical models of communication reign.

We asked our UK customer insights community how they respond to these three stages of advertising. Here's what they have to say...

1. 'Tradvertising': The rejection of traditional advertising - Attention is currency, and consumers are refusing to pay up

75% feel bombarded with advertisements throughout their daily lives, with 74% finding themselves irritated by this incursion on their time. And it's not just a mild disruption, either: 1 in 4 find advertising extremely intrusive, whilst 1 in 2 believe it is somewhat disruptive. Only 7% voted that they are not in any way distracting or troublesome.

There's something to be said for advertising causing disruption as a signpost of it doing its job. The most annoying, repetitive, and intrusive ads may well be the ones we remember. Though provoking a strong reaction is desirable, when an ad causes more irritation than interest, it isn't conducive to brand loyalty.

NINA GLYNN
Ad Blockers, Advertainment, And Advocacy: Why Gen-Z Is Blocking Paid Ads In Favour Of Real Voices

As Craig Davis says, "We need to stop interrupting what people are interested in and be what people are interested in." It's this awareness of being advertised to that is part of the problem. Howard Luck Gossage says, "Nobody reads ads. People read what interests them, and sometimes it's an ad." Hyper-awareness of targeting has made the community shut down, with over half of the Bulbshare community having an ad blocker installed on their browser, and 75% trying their best to avoid ads at any opportunity. And, if there's a skip button on an ad, 99% said they'd be likely to press it, with half specifying they would always skip the ad.

The worst offender was pop-up ads, according to 77%. This was closely followed by social media ads, with the community telling us they must sift through paid endorsements and sponsored posts to see what your friends are doing. Third came TV ads. This exchange of time, data, and attention for access to entertainment and information is at the root of the friction. TV, radio, podcast, social media, and pop-up ads all had a highly negative response rate - whereas billboards and print ads were rated as inoffensive comparatively. An ad that actively interrupts your activity or absorption of stimuli is more of an offence than a static ad on the side of the road or on a page. It is your choice to ignore a picture on the page of the magazine you're reading but being forced to watch an ad to access a video or news article was met with a sense of powerlessness.

Of course, when demanding consumer attention is the end goal, advertising without annoying is like walking a tightrope. As mentioned earlier, $3/4$ of the community make a concerted effort to ignore ads - and 63% have an ad blocker. Similarly, 1 in 3 'always' occupy themselves with another task when TV ads come on, with 62% voting for 'sometimes'. 72% will likely check their phone when adverts come on, 71% head out of the room to the bathroom or to top up their water, and 36% change the channel or mute the TV.

Marketers must balance the patience and goodwill of their audiences with a memorable message that sticks - and this is no easy feat in a world of ad blockers and skip buttons. When attempts to capture attention and mesmerise your target audience are falling flat, is it time to look to alternative routes of marketing?

> "Advertising will die out." Iain, Male, 60
> "I hate advertising. Try to sell me something I don't need. Why? For what gain? Profit! Buy what you really need." Walt, Male, 70

NINA GLYNN
Ad Blockers, Advertainment, And Advocacy:
Why Gen-Z Is Blocking Paid Ads In Favour Of Real Voices

"Ads will go the way of the dodo because they will become non relevant. People skip commercials, block YouTube ads, block internet advertising and so never see most of these ads." Daniel, Male, 49

"If I can skip an ad - why wouldn't I? I want to get past it as quickly as possible so I can continue what I was watching." Maia, Female, 23

2. Advertainment: Blurring boundaries between entertainment and advertising

With half of the community voting that the metaverse will be the next frontier for marketing, and 43% agreeing that gaming is a level up for advertising, the world of advertising is on the brink of a full transition into advertainment. When the lines between advertising and entertainment are blurred, two things happen. One: you achieve what Craig Davis advises - you become what the consumer is interested in rather than interrupting what they're interested in. Two: you overcome the resistance that customers have towards being sold to.

This obfuscation of boundaries between media and marketing has been practised for some time via product placement in movies. These are ads you can't skip or mute. With Reese's Pieces making quite the integral appearance in E.T., Wilson playing best supporting act in *Castaway*, and Tic Tacs being passed around in *Home Alone*, product placement has an established place in mainstream film.

Fossen, writing for The Conversation, says, "While many product placements are the result of paid relationships, some happen because of creative decisions, such as a writer wanting a character to wear Gucci to convey the character's affluence. Viewers aren't typically given information to distinguish between paid and unpaid product placements."

This style of advertising may not be new - but it is sticking around for the future. When done in a way that isn't at Truman Show levels of cringeworthy, it can promote a brand and its values through powerful subliminal messaging. 69% of the community think product placement is effective - but 58% agree that it is only effective when it is done subtly. "I do think advertising is going to be on the internet more than anywhere else and the new metaverse is going to be as well." Jennifer, Female, 39.

NINA GLYNN
Ad Blockers, Advertainment, And Advocacy:
Why Gen-Z Is Blocking Paid Ads In Favour Of Real Voices

> "Product placement works. But ONLY if I can't tell it's happening. If I see a character, I admire in a movie wearing a bag I like, I'll bite, but if there are long drawn out shots of a character sipping a branded beer and the camera lingers on the logo I'm over it!"
> Ellen, Female, 19

3. The dawn and dusk of influencer marketing: Expired trust

Though product placement is age-old, this transition to advertainment accelerated with the rise of the influencer. Consumers are now voluntarily watching ads. YouTubers intwine brand messaging into entertaining videos, soothing the resistance towards being obviously sold to. Hence, 60% say that influencer marketing replaced normal adverts - and 66% think sponsored influencer content muddies the waters between advertising and entertainment.

Of course, this blurring is one that many consumers resist, with fears of an Orwellian appropriation of art and entertainment. In fact, 84% of our insight community say they have lost trust in influencers.

Once upon a time, when Instagram was in its infancy, the dark arts of influencer marketing were a trade secret. Now, the cat is out of the bag. Gen-Z are increasingly sceptical about the transactional relationships that define influencer culture and are wising up to warning signs of inauthenticity: #ad, #sponsored, #prpackage. No longer are users fooled by promises of an aspirational life that will transpire at the click of the affiliate link.

As we've established, when consumers become aware of the tactics used to vie for their money and attention, they become resentful.

> "No I don't really trust them, I think they are only promoting things because they make money or commission from them."
> Bulbshare user, Female, 23
>
> "No, I follow my own thoughts and feelings" Bulbshare user, Female, 47
>
> "No, I like to listen to their thoughts, but never trust them blindly, because they are doing business." Bulbshare user, Male, 36
>
> "I don't... what they are peddling might look good, but comments usually tell a different story."
> Bulbshare user, Female, 28

Ad Blockers, Advertainment, And Advocacy: Why Gen-Z Is Blocking Paid Ads In Favour Of Real Voices

"Self obsessed and untrustworthy individuals who have nothing to do with me." Bulbshare user, Female, 24

"As long as they are being paid they will promote anything." Bulbshare user, Female, 32

"They are good at what they do, but their ultimate goal is to make money from speaking about topics or selling me something. I don't put too much weight into what they say." Bulbshare user, Male, 18

"I don't trust influencers that much because they can be bought over." Bulbshare user, Male, 22

4. Advocacy and authenticity: A snowball effect in marketing

The next frontier, then, is no longer paid endorsements but genuine, authentic recommendations from real people. 86% would be more inclined to buy a product recommended by a friend than a paid influencer.

An army of advocates promoting your product with real fervour is a snowball effect that will go further than any ad. As Facebook's Maloire Lucich says, "People share, read and generally engage more with any type of content when it's surfaced through friends and people they know and trust."

Interestingly, when we asked how the community occupy themselves during a commercial break, half said they chat with their friends or family who they're watching with. And when 66% are more likely to buy a product recommended by their relations over that which has been advertised to them, clearly word of mouth advocacy is the solution to a switched off audience. It comes as no surprise in this post-ad world that 81% trust real opinions over those promoted via an advert.

Authenticity never gets old. Quality never gets old. And when your customers are genuinely excited by your product, they will tell their network about it with a passion that can't be faked. 74% would promote a product they genuinely care about online. Moreover, 88% are enthusiastic about collaborating with brands and 76% said they enjoy reviewing products. When the average consumer has such capacity to become a brand ambassador, it leaves a question mark over the future of paid influencer marketing. With authentic, trusted, unendorsed voices shouting about your brand in customer communities and beyond, there is little need to resort to paid opinion.

NINA GLYNN
Ad Blockers, Advertainment, And Advocacy: Why Gen-Z Is Blocking Paid Ads In Favour Of Real Voices

As Forbes says[1], "Loyalty—consistent customers who make repeat purchases—is a great thing to achieve. [...] But loyalty has its limits. It doesn't spread exponentially. [...] Advocacy is different. When clients become advocates, they're out there promoting us on their own. [...]

Perhaps, for example, you hear that a colleague is considering pursuing a certain type of consulting service, and you tell them, "You might want to try Firm A because we had a great experience with them. Again, no one asked you to do that, you just did it on your own—when the opportunity arose."

We've seen traditional advertising. We've even seen advertainment. Now, we're stepping into new possibilities. Forget TV, billboards, podcasts, social media - the next conduit of your brand message is your customer.

> "I am a firm believer in word of mouth advertisement." - Taynelle, Female, 45
>
> "I think gone are the days when you see the latest film's advertising on bus stops." Alison, Female, 49
>
> "I never take notice of influencers at all and prefer to make my own purchase decisions or recommendations from family." Bulbshare user, Male, 25
>
> "To me, brand advocacy is having a great feeling about a brand because of who they are and sharing that with others." Bulbshare user, Female, 30

5. UGC - Masters of advocacy: L'Oréal case study

As The Guardian says[2], "Advertising is failure. Ideally, a company offers a great product or service that its customers love, talk about, and sell to each other. It's when that fails that you need to advertise."

More and more brands are turning to UGC to add zest to their marketing campaigns, build meaningful relationships, and create relatable content that customers love. And Covid-19 only accelerated this: the connection and entertainment that UGC offers made it uniquely popular during lockdowns, with 78% of our customers spending more time online.

---

[1] https://www.forbes.com/sites/forbesmarketplace/2022/02/08/from-loyalty-to-advocacy-the-key-to-effective-customer-experience/?sh=3acdb9407393

[2] https://www.theguardian.com/media/organgrinder/2009/jun/08/user-generated-content-internet-media

NINA GLYNN
Ad Blockers, Advertainment, And Advocacy: Why Gen-Z Is Blocking Paid Ads In Favour Of Real Voices

The Drum agrees[3]: "Brands have been pushed to find alternative solutions to complex studio setups, huge budgets and high production value – all of the traditional expectations for an impactful advertising campaign. A strategy that's found success is the clever utilisation of user-generated content (UGC) as it taps into a real desire for human connection, strengthens a community and, in this unprecedented time, has transformed what might have once been local content into global content."

Shopping experiences became unrecognisable during Covid – especially for makeup. And in a world where the customer can't try their foundation before buying it, makeup retailers such as L'Oréal have been presented with an obstacle to overcome. But the L'Oréal brand, NYX Professional Makeup, saw an opportunity in this obstacle.

NYX Professional Makeup launched Makeup ADDYX, their customer insight and product testing community with Bulbshare, amidst the pandemic to roaring success. Within this app of makeup lovers, NYX Professional Makeup co-created their CAN'T STOP WON'T STOP ALL THE OBSESSION tagline for their popular foundation. Hoping to leverage the powerful consumer love for the Can't Stop Won't Stop foundation – despite the lack of testers – the makeup brand pursued the route of reviews, UGC, and insights to create authentic buzz.

To overcome the testers hurdle, NYX Professional Makeup guided consumers to their website, where they could choose their shade based on swatch imagery and a variety of model pictures. Having sent bottles of the product to the community to try, NYX Professional Makeup used consumer insights to inspire the new hook of their campaign – as well as the messaging, look and feel, and imagery.

The project drove rich UGC, including before and after photos, application shots, final images of them holding the bottle, short video clips of consumers raving about the foundation, realistic images of the wear and tear of longevity after a long day, and creative TikTok style transitions. Additionally, consumers sent in ratings and reviews which could be promulgated in their social media and campaigns.

Combining the power of UGC and product insights, they moulded a campaign which had the consumer at its core, every step of the way.

---

3 https://www.thedrum.com/opinion/2020/06/04/why-ugc-exploding-popularity-among-brands-during-covid-19

NINA GLYNN
Ad Blockers, Advertainment, And Advocacy:
Why Gen-Z Is Blocking Paid Ads In Favour Of Real Voices

With hundreds of videos and images to utilise, and a social sharing reach of 70,000+, the Can't Stop Won't Stop is a resounding example of UGC done right.

> *"User generated content is a brilliant tool with which to connect to your customers. It invites them in to become a crucial part of the branding process and makes them feel part of something big - which increases brand loyalty. With this campaign, we saw some amazing results and we loved all the images and videos the tribe sent in. We'll definitely continue to put our customers at the core."*
>
> **Meg Grant, Assistant Product Manager, L'Oréal UK & Ireland**

> *"UGC formed a powerful driver for the Can't Stop Won't Stop campaign. With rich imagery and video content galore, the Makeup Addyx app fuelled the look and feel and injected some serious authenticity, passion, and fun into the marketing of the foundation. By putting the consumers at the heart of everything, we harnessed the brand love around the product and inspired even more."*
>
> **Roxanne Smith, Client Collaborator and lead on the L'Oréal UK & Ireland account, Bulbshare**

For more inspiration see cases studies for NYX Professional Makeup[4], eBay[5], and Voxi[6].

N.B. The Bulbshare community is a Gen-Pop sample of 1,792 participants from the UK, made up of 35% of 16-25 year olds, 50% of 26-50 year olds, and 15% of 51+ year olds. They filtered to under-25 for Gen-Z specific information. The participants are made up of 63% women, 34% men, and 3% non-binary participants. The information was gathered through surveys with multiple-choice questions and open text response boxes.

Nina Glynn is the Senior Content Manager at Bulbshare. She works on content, copywriting, social media and marketing communications. Nina has written copy for some leading brands including, L'Oreal, PHE, Asahi, Depop, Nestlé and AB InBev.

---

[4] https://bulbshare.com/en/casestudies/csws/
[5] https://bulbshare.com/en/casestudies/ebay/
[6] https://bulbshare.com/en/casestudies/voxi/

MELANIE LOEPER & MEGAN TANDY
What Branded Content Campaigns Can Learn From Sports Sponsorship Data Analysis

We at IRIS are passionate about sports. Football, equestrian, volleyball – you name it. Not only do we love sports though - we also love data. Ever since our foundation in 2014 we have been proving ourselves as experts when it comes to data-driven analysis and evaluation of sports-related sponsorships.

Measuring sponsorship effects is a fulfilling task because if sponsorship is done right, the return-on-investment can be immense. It is not a new form of marketing and yet it still seems to offer endless opportunities, being both highly adaptive and innovative. Additionally, sponsorships partially paved the way for a branded content and influencer marketing mindset. It demonstrated early on that you do not necessarily have to talk about your product to promote it. Branded content, influencer marketing and sponsorships have one big common denominator: they are all trying to avoid a sales tone and instead want to connect to the consumer on an emotional level to be associated with a certain feeling, lifestyle etc.

Sponsorships are an incredibly effective way of advertising. You can get your name out there, slowly but steadily sticking in the minds of your audience. Generally, brands try to sponsor clubs or athletes with shared values and select their partners carefully. Clubs with an outstandingly positive image usually have a spill-over effect on sponsors. That way, everybody wins. Viewers are not bothered with long commercial breaks; clubs have a stable income pillar, and the brand gets more popular.

And yet, sponsoring effects are evident. Brand awareness and popularity are almost always higher among people aware of a sponsorship compared to people unaware of a sponsorship. Likewise, supporters of a club are usually more likely to consider and buy products of a brand that is sponsoring their team compared to the general population. Most of the times, the build-up of brand awareness and image via sponsoring takes time and patience. Your brand will not double its KPIs overnight. Endurance is key though: eventually, the brand will achieve significantly higher numbers - without risking negative backlashes from the audience as we sometimes experience with classical marketing tools such as commercial ads.

MELANIE LOEPER & MEGAN TANDY
What Branded Content Campaigns Can Learn From Sports Sponsorship Data Analysis

At IRIS we're continuously working on expanding our horizons. And we came to realise: if branded content, influencer marketing and sponsorships are so closely related, why not adapt our powerful tools to the measurement of marketing beyond the realm of sports? After all, the core concept of both sponsorships, branded content and influencer marketing is the same: a somewhat restrained yet well-thought-out approach to target your consumer audience. Staying in people's mind without aggressively confronting them with your brand.

The Austrian energy drink company Red Bull is a master of both worlds. They successfully established a sponsorship structure across several sports, with entire clubs and teams advocating their brand – and even winning trophies along the way, like Max Verstappen in Formula 1™ or German Football Cup winners RB Leipzig.

Arguably, Red Bull managed to create a hybrid of sponsorship and branded content. They are directing clubs and teams that first and foremost practice their sport and do not promote the brand verbally. However, since the clubs and teams are deeply connected to Red Bull as a company, it is not a classical sponsorship in which a sponsor wouldn't get to have a say about club politics for example. Paradoxically, it is both an external sponsorship and an in-house production of branded content. Nonetheless, Red Bull is also a champion of *classical* branded content. They have countless extreme sports formats such as Red Bull Rampage or Red Bull Joyride which can be streamed on their website. When we measure the impact of branded content like this on the target audience, it becomes obvious how powerful this marketing strategy is.

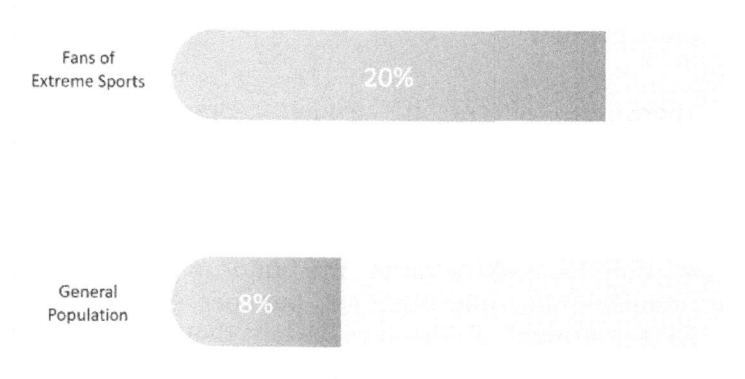

Fans of Extreme Sports: 20%

General Population: 8%

Illustration 2: Consideration of Red Bull in the US among fans of extreme sports vs. general population (Source: IRIS Syndicated Database)

MELANIE LOEPER & MEGAN TANDY
What Branded Content Campaigns Can Learn From Sports Sponsorship Data Analysis

Sports don't necessarily need to be involved for us to be passionate about tracking marketing effects though. Let's delve into a completely different success story: Shein - The Chinese fast fashion company was founded only 14-years ago and managed to gain popularity quickly – mostly amongst female teenagers outside of China. Shein's marketing strategy is mostly reliant on social media.

Both popular influencers and smaller users in terms of followership include Shein's products in their Instagram reels and TikTok posts. Simultaneously, Shein is forecasting the fashion of tomorrow with the help of algorithms that calculate emerging trends as they are happening. Shein is mastering the inclusion of their audience into their marketing while always being one step ahead of the consumers. Since they are committed so much to social media, it doesn't come as a surprise that Instagram and Tik Tok users are much more aware of the brand compared to the general population.

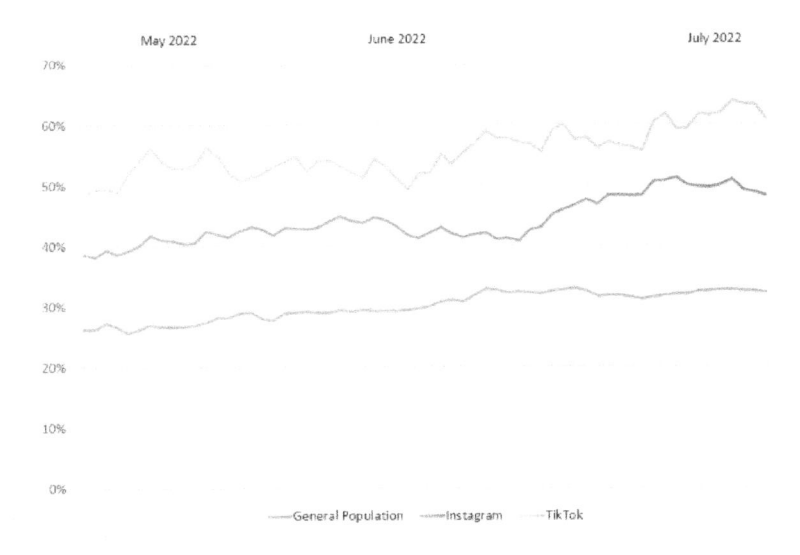

Illustration 3: Brand Awareness of Shein throughout May-July 2022 in the US among the general population, Instagram users and TikTok users (Source: IRIS Syndicated Database)

Branded content and influencer marketing might look easy at first glance. It is not. You must know your target group very well to choose the right format, style, and topic for your marketing campaign. That's why we at IRIS are so ardent about data analysis. It allows you to deeply understand the preferences of your (potential) consumers before you reach out to them and possibly put your marketing budget at risk. What do they like? What do they dislike? Which media channels do the use? How do they feel about trends and recent developments?

MELANIE LOEPER & MEGAN TANDY
What Branded Content Campaigns Can Learn From Sports Sponsorship Data Analysis

Over the past few years, we have seen how much of a difference data analysis can make to implement successful sponsorships.

We will see it for branded content as well.

Melanie Loeper is Account Manager at IRIS Sport. She is a market researcher with work experience in the FMCG and sports industry. Her primary focus is the football industry, working both with sponsors and clubs to assess sponsorships and conduct data analyses, target group analyses and brand performance tracking.

Megan Tandy is Sales Manager at IRIS Sport. She was born and raised in northern BC, Canada. After a 15-year career as a professional biathlete, including 3 Olympic Games, Megan now works in the Sport Sponsorship industry. You can find her working with a wide range of brands, federations and organisations to optimise their sponsorship engagements.

STEFANO MARRONE
Why Animation Is The Best Way To Campaign About Sensitive Topics

Marketers often forget that content creation and entertainment are inextricably linked. At the end of the day, people consume content for only two reasons: if it's informative and if it's entertaining. The ultimate achievement for branded content creators is to manage to be both at the same time.

There are content topics, though, where the entertainment aspect needs to be handled carefully. As creatives and storytellers with clients such as charities and pharma companies, we constantly ask ourselves how to tackle campaigns that revolve around sensitive topics such as abuse of physical and psychological kind, humanitarian emergencies, dramatic medical conditions.

For a relevant example, let's delve into Nucco's award-winning campaign "Wildlife. Not entertainers" with World Animal Protection (WAP), which resulted in more than half a million petitions signed and an increased awareness on specific instances of animal cruelty[1], as well as winning various awards, such as The People's Choice Award at The World Responsible Awards.

We think that sharing some of the challenges we encountered on the project can give interesting insights and tools on how to work with delicate topics.

World Animal Protection asked for Nucco's help to create a powerful visual story to highlight their plight against the use of elephants in the tourism/entertainment industry, and elephant rides in particular.

Having worked for years on campaigns to protect endangered animals worldwide, the World Animal Protection marketing team had a clear idea on how to handle sensitive topics, especially on the side of wording. Our job was to translate that sensibility into visual storytelling, while working on the main campaign film, as well as creating various visual assets in digital and print.

---

1 https://www.worldanimalprotection.org/wildlife-not-entertainers

STEFANO MARRONE
Why Animation Is The Best Way To Campaign About Sensitive Topics

The main campaign film follows the life of an African elephant. Her sad fate is sealed when her parents are killed by poachers and she, still a calf, is caged then sold to perform tourist rides. The film then explains how people from all over the world are unwittingly contributing to a life of animal slavery. There's no happy ending, just the profound realisation that this is going to be her life forever.

Thanks to our close collaboration with WAP, we managed to avoid some tricky traps along the path of deciding how to show the distress of elephants held captive and abused in the tourism/entertainment industry.

1. Dealing with graphic imagery

When working on a campaign focused on a sensitive topic, there's always a 'shock card' that can be played: show graphical images to get an immediate emotional reaction from the audience.

However, this technique can be a double-edged sword. Regardless of how sensitive the audience can be towards the issue that the campaign is trying to tackle, individuals can be so affected by graphical images that they might shy away from taking action. Everybody's sensitivity is set on a different level and can result in an opposite reaction to a desired one.

During our first brainstorming with the WAP team, we knew that scenes of direct violence on the elephants were to be avoided, favouring an approach that would focus on empathy and on visual and audio hints to imply violence, without showing it.

2. Fighting emotional distance

The other issue associated with the use of the 'shock card' is related to the human tendency to establish as much distance as possible from images that depict an unhealthy situation. That's how we are biologically wired: we see disease and undesirable images and the immediate reaction is to start drawing an imaginary line between 'me' and 'what I am seeing'.

We wanted to avoid subconscious inner dialogues of this kind: "This issue is happening in Africa and India, not in my country, why should I be concerned?" A little switch is activated in our brain that tries to put a barrier between us and the problems that are presented in front of our eyes; it's a short-term survival instinct.

STEFANO MARRONE
Why Animation Is The Best Way To Campaign About Sensitive Topics

"Get as far as you can from this issue, create some distance" is what the brain is suggesting us to do.

Our solution was to leave violence 'out-of-the-picture', allowing each viewer to apply their level of sensitivity and imagination to the story they're watching. This approach has a very powerful reaction in the viewer's mind: the violent or shocking activity - implied and not shown - is as strong as the audience can take.

Most Oscar Wilde critics agree that the first edition of "The Picture of Dorian Gray" is the most intriguing compared to the following ones because Dorian's malicious acts are not explained in detail: he is as evil and corrupted as the readers wants him to be. Great cinema is full of brilliant examples of implied violence too. In the 1996 film *Sleepers*, Director Barry Levinson lets our imagination run wild while the camera slowly pans away from the reform school vault where terrible acts of violence are taking place. This is why the animation team of Nucco has deliberately left any violent act off-screen - like the shooting of the young elephant parents. We see the consequences of the violence, never the violence itself.

3. Applying the power of stylisation

By stylisation, we mean a deliberate design choice to eliminate all unnecessary visual information that can divert the audience attention away from the key message we want to communicate.

STEFANO MARRONE
Why Animation Is The Best Way To Campaign About Sensitive Topics

Colette Collins, Deputy Director of Communications at World Animal Protection puts it very clearly:

> **"We chose to tell our story through an animation to convey this complex issue in a simple way."**

The "simple way" she refers to is exactly what makes animation so powerful.

The WAP animated film is extremely expressive thanks to stylization: we focused on the main protagonist, a female baby elephant, and told her story in a powerful, stylised way, in which one scene is connected to the other by using emotional transitions that allow the audience to engage with a strong level of empathy. Stylised images are more powerful because they break the barrier of specificity and hit the chords of empathy.

The animation team used this technique to get the best possible result. They wanted to convey what happens to the elephants behind the curtains, before the show starts, without being specific or graphical about it. That's why they kept the baby elephant, after they were taken away from his mum, always under a spotlight, as if they were constantly part of the attraction.

The campaign film has a strong resemblance to old puppet shows: the use of silhouettes and watercolours transitions gives it a special melancholic feeling. This aesthetic approach, allowed us to be extremely expressive, sensitive, and poetic with this story, touching the audience in the deepest way.

4. Leverage empathy

There is a reason why animated films, comics and cartoons are the entertainment products that more easily spread across different markets. Think about how much manga and anime content are international successes against live-action Japanese films, for example, or how many more international phenomena are stylised content.

When you selectively take away specificity from an image through stylisation, it becomes more universal. A stylised character is more like the idea that the viewer has of him/herself. By choosing which elements to stress on a character, a visual storyteller can make the content he is working on broad, in terms of empathy.

STEFANO MARRONE
Why Animation Is The Best Way To Campaign About Sensitive Topics

Think about the smiley, its simplicity enables it to depict virtually every face on Earth: two eyes and a mouth, everybody has them, so we are the smiley. If you want to explore this concept further, Scott McCloud talks extensively about it in the second chapter of his book, *Understanding Comics: The Invisible Art*[2].

5. Create immediacy

As a marketer, brand manager or product owner, the need of creating a message that is straight to the point and effective in an era of super-quick interaction is paramount.

Stylisation and its expression in motion - animation - allow for that immediacy, together with an immediate visual association with the branding visual elements. We can be deliberate from the very first frame, building a visual world that reflects the brand values with absolute precision, and with way less budgets restrictions as opposed to the live-action (and ample CGI) version of the same story.

> *"With this animation we can educate and open up the public's eyes to the cruelty behind elephant riding, and to inspire them to be a part of the solution to help end the cruelty."*
> **Colette Collins, Deputy Director of Communications, World Animal Protection**

---

[2] *Understanding Comics: The Invisible Art* by Scott McCloud, Tundra Publishing, 1993

STEFANO MARRONE
Why Animation Is The Best Way To Campaign About Sensitive Topics

Closing thoughts

Striking the right balance when it comes to sensitive topics in branded content is not easy, but when the right storytelling approach is applied, the results can be profound.

When dealing with sensitive topics, the immediacy and iconic power of animation inspires empathy, the most powerful of human triggers, bringing people emotionally close to the action, while getting rid of all the avoidance traps that our brain creates to ward off facing difficult topics and hard truths. If the storytelling is compelling enough, even if what people see is ugly, the mirror will hold.

Stefano Marrone is a Partner at Unit9, a global production partner with offices in Los Angeles, New York, London, Berlin and Lodz. He also founded Nucco, a communication and experience expert that change behaviour and perspectives for brands. Stefano is also a Partner and NED for Book on a Tree - a storytelling hub for writers all over Europe. He supports the company board and managers in critical strategic decision-making and planning; He enjoys working on art direction of comic books and graphic novel projects for publishers such as Planeta DeAgostini, Disney Publishing, Penguin Random House and Rizzoli. Stefano is a mentor of start-ups in marketing and branding for Google for Startups, where he is a Lead Marketing Mentor and Keynote Speaker; as well as a guest-lecture at various universities in Europe, including, ESCP, Goldsmiths, NABA, SOAS and UCL.

SANDRA FREISINGER-HEINL & CHRISTINA KUFER
Green Advertising And Content In Germany

The colour 'green' has experienced quite a boom during the last few years. 'Green' is a colour with which we associate a healthy lifestyle. On top of that, shades of green are the most regularly clicked colour schemes by advertisers, see Shutterstock study in 20 countries 2022[1].

For many of us 'green' is more than a colour. It is symbol of natural growth and of sustainability. 'Green' can be a way of life. In Germany there even is a government party with that name, 'Die Grünen' (The Green Ones). But 'green' is also a promise, one that brands and productions give in their advertisement and have to keep – morally and legally.

Which concrete requirements for companies result from producing 'Green Advertising and Content' for their brands? On the one hand, we will be examining which recent content is produced at the moment, and on the other hand, what legal conditions have to be met - with examples from experience as well as checklists.

Green Advertising & Content Enables Brands and Productions to Demonstrate Standing

Five important factors we have identified in relation to Green Advertising and Content mirror in their content the brands and productions' ambitions but also the challenges they are facing.

1. Emotional experiences

How do I render the topics climate change, environmental protection and sustainability so that they can be emotionally experienced by the young target group? And how do I bring them close to as many young people as possible? For this purpose, the TV production i&u (Leonine Studios) went an unusual way with the science influencer Jacob Beautemps and three years ago realised the first *YouTopia*.

---

[1] https://www.wuv.de/Archiv/Shutterstock-Das-sind-die-Farbtrends-2022

SANDRA FREISINGER-HEINL & CHRISTINA KUFER
Green Advertising And Content In Germany

Once a year, five influencers move in under a large dome for four days in order to discuss important topics of our time: climate change, environmental protection and sustainability. *"YouTopia* is one of Germany's biggest digital events", explains Henrik Wittmann, Head of Digital at the production company i&u TV in Cologne – speaking at the BCMA x SKW Schwarz Branded Content Lunch Talk[2] – and in the meantime, it has been adapted internationally. Last year it went ahead in France. 101 million contacts were achieved through *YouTopia* in Germany last year.

The influencers are streaming 'non-stop' live on their own channels via YouTube and Twitch and are designing a varied program with more than 50 other influencers and celebrities from TV, politics as well as science. There are experiments, talks and videos, but also entertainment-highlights, such as, late night shows and live concerts. *YouTopia* is financed by brands who are positioning themselves within the Gen-Z environment.

Influencers at the YouTopia Dome

---
2 https://www.youtube.com/watch?v=6S3lkDdrabE&t=4s

SANDRA FREISINGER-HEINL & CHRISTINA KUFER
Green Advertising And Content In Germany

2. Being authentic

The colour green on its own doesn't yet bring sustainability. In order to win credibility a company has to act 'green' in their advertising. "Green advertising is only then authentic if sustainability is at the core of the corporate strategy", says Christina Niedermaier, Head of Content Marketing, E.ON Germany (see Branded Content Lunch Talk). Because of that the most important aspect in the company's strategy are the ideas #DasWirbewegtmehr (together we can achieve more) and everyone can be a #changemaker. This is how E.ON in the last few years, during very difficult times for any energy corporation, developed from a traditional electricity and gas supplier towards a sustainable solution provider. They communicate this not only through its product portfolio but also through its promotional activities.

The electricity supplier makes sure that all measures, throughout all channels, are climate-neutral. For their product advertisement campaign on e-mobility with the slogan 'Sauber laden, Sauber fahren' (Clean charging, clean driving), which is placed on traditional media plus digital, ClimatePartner, together with their media agency, calculates the CO_2 emissions. According to this amount, new trees are planted. E.ON itself bought land for this forest in which employees also participate actively. This shows that everyone is serious.

E.ON's campaign 'Sauber Laden, sauber fahren' (Clean charging, clean driving)

SANDRA FREISINGER-HEINL & CHRISTINA KUFER
Green Advertising And Content In Germany

Another example from content communication is the Future Energy Home by influencer Thore Schölermann[3]. Thore and E.ON created a *nachhaltige Energiewelt* (a sustainable energy world). Thore's house has been designed with solar panels on the flat roof, heat pump and wall box in the garage. As for the construction itself great value has been attached to sustainable materials. This way E.ON managed to create a content world for a sustainable energy future in which product communication for significant E.ON products was realised. In addition, E.ON recently launched its own YouTube channel on e-mobility, *Electrip* powered by E.ON[4].

Thore's sustainable energy world

3. Reducing carbon footprint

We often find ourselves talking about what every single one of us can do in order to reduce our carbon footprint. Food retailer REWE has even established a new expression for all its green initiatives: The expression 'undenkbar' (unthinkable) is transformed into #umdenkbar (re-thinkable). This hashtag is not only a new campaign umbrella, but it results in real actions too: REWE expanded its organic as well as regional product range, and eliminated the plastic wrapping for fruit and vegetables, abolished magazines made out of paper and created internal initiatives. This is very fitting for the brand, given that nutrition is one of the most important factors involved in their annual CO_2 emissions[5]. REWE feels responsible and wants to be part of the solution themselves, as is shown by its numerous actions.

---
3 https://www.youtube.com/watch?v=1ulLt2SOOgI
4 https://www.youtube.com/channel/UCcaKUZZKN5z-QCizTil5Z5Q
5 https://www.wuv.de/Themen/Markenstrategie/Rewe-spendet-25-Millionen-Euro-fuer-den-Klimaschutz

SANDRA FREISINGER-HEINL & CHRISTINA KUFER
Green Advertising And Content In Germany

In the next five years REWE is going to donate a total of 25 million euros to climate protection. With this money the supermarket chain supports the newly founded climate fund 'Nabu' of the 'Bund Naturschutz e.V.' The label of 'Nabu' will be present on the private labels 'REWE Bio' (REWE organic) and 'REWE Beste Wahl' (REWE best choice).

Posters which clean polluted air through a special coating have been installed at prominent places in Cologne, Frankfurt, Hamburg, Berlin, Leipzig and Munich.

Last but not least, REWE also directs its influencer and content strategy accordingly: Thus REWE will, for example, be partner of *YouTopia* this year and is going to deliver vegan groceries.

Within the framework of these efforts REWE additionally made use of the possibility of digital product placement in RTL dailies such as *Gute Zeiten, Schlechte Zeiten* (Good times, bad times). This series is produced in green production and offers a sustainable TV environment for product placement. By using the artificial intelligence technology of Mirriad, posters with the hashtag #umdenkbar have been integrated into the content in completed episodes.

4. Going beyond limits

By now companies even dare to rattle the old boundaries' cage and to look outside the box. Social pressure is increasing and the transport industry provides us with many novelties. Electrical mobility picks up speed very quickly in the car industry. Parallel to this development we have bicycle roads in Germany where bikes have priority over cars. Likewise Uber, e-scooters and car-sharing go down well now with the majority of the population and currently there even exists a monthly ticket for public transport which only costs 9 EUR.

The car brand Toyota ventures into this territory with their campaign 'Beyond Zero' for hydrogen cars which don't leave behind emissions. It states on the website hub[6], "How would you enjoy a world in which your mobility leaves behind null emissions". Furthermore, in the video *Toyotas Woven City* the company introduced the animated prototype of a 'City of the Future' in which you can live in harmony with nature[7]. This city will be built in Japan.

---

6 https://www.toyota.de/entdecke-toyota/beyond-zero?gclid=Cj0KCQjwuaiXBhCCARIsAKZLt3mgahc-weCN84G-tkfKPH4KJWAo_Jawl89RPZi9QEadkk-Zv0WATQoaAuMPEALw_wcB&gclsrc=aw.ds
7 https://www.youtube.com/watch?v=ng3X39lenvg

SANDRA FREISINGER-HEINL & CHRISTINA KUFER
Green Advertising And Content In Germany

Toyota additionally carried out the 'Fuel Cell Talks' at *YouTopia* with influencers and experts on mobility, innovation and society of the future which are now on their website too.

In order to avoid getting too serious: let's finish with an amusing content example of the car producer. Toyota carried out a very special challenge with its model Prius in collaboration with influencers. The Prius was the world's first hybrid car that has been mass-produced and is therefore an icon. The influencers Lisa Küppers and Jonas Ems announced a competition in a Prius[8].

This contest was not about who makes it from A to B the fastest, but instead it was evaluated who was driving electrically the most. During this competition the two influencers additionally had to master a karaoke challenge.

5. Go for good: in both microcosm and macrocosm

It is only reasonable to become involved on a small or on a large scale, because everything makes a difference. Even through smaller campaigns with great attention to detail brands are able to deliver interesting information to their consumers and to generate exciting content. One brand who does both is Vodafone.

On a very large scale, Vodafone creates content which uses the hashtag #Gigagreen that all networks in Europe and therefore also all Vodafone connections that clients use are run on electricity from sustainable sources[9].

The TV spot of the mutual campaign with Apple for iPhone 13 #LoveShareProtect[10] has been produced 'climate-friendly' and 'climate-neutrally'. It was filmed in Slovenia, a country which could be reached by train. The number of participants on set was reduced from 100 to 25. No plastic foil and generators were used, costumes only rented and shooting happened with natural light, as is evident in the behind-the-scenes-content[11]. Vodafone is talking about a third less CO_2 emission compared to conventional filming of a commercial spot and has compensated for the remaining two thirds[12].

---

8 https://www.youtube.com/watch?v=xsTfyB5vilA
9 https://www.vodafone.de/featured/inside-vodafone/alles-auf-gigagreen-die-vodafone-netze-in-europa-funken-mit-100-prozent-gruenem-strom/
10 https://www.youtube.com/watch?v=r2SFgFYPGCg&feature=emb_rel_end
11 https://www.youtube.com/watch?v=GurDsDgSrBw
12 https://www.horizont.net/marketing/nachrichten/kampagne-von-vodafone-und-apple-so-geht-nachhaltige-tv-werbung-195597

SANDRA FREISINGER-HEINL & CHRISTINA KUFER
Green Advertising And Content In Germany

On a smaller scale, Vodafone relies on important and eye-catching topics, for example the protection of bees and increased biodiversity. Therefore, they've moved bees onto the roof of the Vodafone campus. The bees can be watched via cameras in the beehives. Vodafone also contributes to ensuring that the beehives won't be stolen: With the smart device *Giga Bee Protect Box*, Vodafone shows the location of the beehives via information from the Vodafone network. Vodafone also produced content on this topic[13] and furthermore reported on this at *YouTopia's Giga Bee-Talk*.

The fine line between green advertising and misleading greenwashing

However, authentic green advertising does not only mean moral and entrepreneurial authenticity. Green claims must also be authentic from a legal perspective - in other words, they must not mislead consumers and the overall public under the standards of unfair competition. Hence, the crucial question that each company and each advertiser must ask themselves is: Where is the red line to legally impermissible greenwashing?

Current figures from the EU Commission show that this 'red line' is still a big unknown for many companies. While in 2021, 80% of European online shops contained green claims such as 'climate neutral', 'green', 'sustainable' or 'recycled', 42% of the green claims examined in an official EU-wide study were misleading according to current legal standards.

1. The legal requirements in Germany, France and the UK

Under German law (sec. 5 of the Unfair Competition Act), green claims are misleading if they contain untrue statements or other statements capable of deception. The decisive factor is how the addressed public, i.e. in particular, consumers, understand a certain advertising statement. What do consumers, for example, imagine climate neutral gummy bears to be, or a 100% recycled plastic bottle? Subsequently, the question arises whether this so-called understanding of the addressed public corresponds to reality and the actual conditions of a product, service or company. If this is not the case, then an advertisement is typically misleading.

---

13 https://www.youtube.com/watch?v=UEuJsTfRAqU

Similar to health-related advertising, the German courts apply a particularly strict standard. The reason behind this is the special emotional advertising effect that emanates from green advertising and which is particularly likely to mislead consumers. Vague and imprecise environmental statements such as 'eco-friendly' or 'sustainable' should therefore, be viewed with particular caution. As each claim is considered individually and the various courts often have different views, there is, unfortunately, still a great deal of legal uncertainty at present. However, companies can reduce the legal risks by critically examining their green claims regarding their truth and by providing additional background information on their meaning in the advertising material (e.g. so called Asterisk hints *).

Even though the German approach may seem quite strict, other countries are even stricter when it comes to green advertising. In France for example, companies face a fine of up to 80% of the false advertising campaign costs for misleading green statements. As of this year, it will be mandatory to refer to more environmentally friendly alternatives in car advertisements. And from 2023, it will also be forbidden to advertise the climate neutrality of products or services without informing the public about the balance of greenhouse gas emissions and the approach and modalities of reduction or compensation thereof.

Similarly, the UK Competition and Markets Authority (CMA) adopted a Green Claims Code in 2021 and has started to review certain sectors, focusing for the beginning on textiles and fashion, travel and transport and fast-moving consumer goods (FMCG).

2. Current examples from German case law

Germany has seen quite some greenwashing 'shitstorms' in the past few months: from 100% recycled bag packs (Gotbag), which were only somewhat recycled to face masks sold by prominent sustainability influencer Fynn Kliemann, which were allegedly fairly produced in Europe but actually originated from factories in South East Asia.

The legal cases, to date, often revolve around the claim 'climate-neutral' which has occupied numerous German courts in the past two years. Consumer protection organisations such as Verbraucherzentrale and Deutsche Umwelthilfe have taken up the fight against greenwashing and are taking massive legal action against advertisers these days. The latter one for example initiated legal proceedings against Rossmann, DM, Shell, Beiersdorf and BP concerning the claim 'climate-neutral'.

SANDRA FREISINGER-HEINL & CHRISTINA KUFER
Green Advertising And Content In Germany

According to the consumer protection organisations and many German courts, that claim is misleading if it is not explained in the advertising itself that the climate neutrality of the product or service is only achieved by compensation with CO_2 certificates.

Recently, however, the German Higher Regional Court of Schleswig-Holstein ruled that the claim can be admissible even without additional informative notes, because the public may well imagine climate-neutral products to be only compensated products and not just products produced completely CO_2-free.

This shows the current legal uncertainty and it remains to be seen how the Federal Court of Justice will rule here one day in the future.

3. Outlook: The EU Commission's anti-greenwashing plans

Such a ruling is likely to be influenced by the newest anti-greenwashing plans presented by the EU Commission in March 2022. Its goal is to protect consumers from misleading green claims and to make the EU climate-neutral until 2050.

The package contains various measures and is currently debated in the EU institutions. One aspect is that blanket and vague environmental claims, where the excellent environmental performance of the product or company cannot be proven, are to be prohibited per se in the future.

This includes claims such as 'environmentally friendly', 'ecological', 'green', 'climate-neutral' or 'energy efficient'. Environmental claims about the entire product should also be prohibited if they only apply to a partial aspect of the product, as well as voluntary sustainability seals that are not based on a testing procedure by an independent third party or public body.

The EU Commission's proposals are a first step towards even stricter regulation of green advertising at EU level.

4. Checklist for marketing professionals and brands

The examples from case law and the plans of the EU Commission show that there is currently still a great deal of legal uncertainty in the area of green advertising. In any case, companies should not simply use green advertising claims without thinking.

SANDRA FREISINGER-HEINL & CHRISTINA KUFER
Green Advertising And Content In Germany

The following checklist can help to reduce the risk of misleading statements and the potential for greenwashing:

- **Is the green claim objectively correct (and not exaggerated or only half the truth)?**
- **Can I also prove this in court with meaningful evidence?**
- **Does the green claim refer to the entire campaign/product/ service or only to individual aspects thereof?**
- **In the case of vague green claims: Can the claim actually be related to the entire production and delivery process?**
- **Do I need to supplement the green claim with additional information, for example in an 'Asterix note'?**

One thing is certain: Green claims have become indispensable in advertising and branded content. No wonder, since consumers are becoming increasingly environmentally conscious and also take climate change into account in their purchasing decisions. In all this, it is particularly important for companies and brands that they are both authentic in 'green' advertising and content, closely observing the extensive legal rules which apply to 'green' advertising.

Sandra Freisinger-Heinl is Managing Director of Brandplace GmbH, Munich. She is passionate about the branded content industry, she has been conveying the messages of brands and companies in an entertaining and informative way for over 20-years, especially in the digital sector and social media. Sandra is Chairwoman of BCMA DACH (Germany, Austria, Switzerland) and a member of the BCMA Global Council.

Christina Kufer is an Associate at SKW Schwarz Media Lawyers, Munich and advises national and international companies on all aspects of intellectual property rights and in the field of information technology and digital business. Her main areas of expertise include legal support in the design of products and marketing campaigns, the drafting of license and distribution agreements, and advice on the introduction of innovative business models. In addition, she represents start-ups, medium-sized companies and international corporations in extrajudicial and judicial disputes concerning trademarks, designs and copyrights as well as in the field of competition law.

PATRICIA WEISS
Brand Storytelling And Branded Content: The Powerful Meeting Between People's Truth And The Brand's Truth

The harsh truth is: stories are shared because audiences find them interesting, not because they belong to a brand. And probably, the brands' biggest challenge in the present day is how to captivate and get the attention and the time of today's dispersive and distracted audiences.

But the solution isn't simply giving up on communication that's intrusive, such as advertising or content full of marketing, to invest in Branded Content incorporating storytelling, because if there isn't a great and relevant idea and talent behind it, forms and techniques become useless. People connect their emotions with stories that are carried with human values and relate to them.

And above all, the brand story must follow three essential drives: focus on people, relevance and truth.

Brands need to make their first switch, their first key turning point by choosing to tell meaningful stories, which isn't interruptive but is completely focused on the audience.

Where the hero and protagonist are the audiences - not brands - and the focus is not on impact or 'views' and 'likes' but on provoking and expanding a relevant conversation with society, leaving a positive legacy.

Relevance in fact, is a word that seems so obvious as it is rare within our polluted reality caused by so many uninteresting messages, with many brands bombarding consumers around the world every day. Messages that are often irrelevant and overly focused on what brands want to say about them and not about what's interesting and concerns people.

I often say that the true revolution of marketing happens when brands really step into people's shoes. Because no brand will find it's own truth and also people's truth if this 'displacement' doesn't happen, transforming it's mindset and transcending it's point of view.

PATRICIA WEISS
Brand Storytelling And Branded Content: The Powerful Meeting Between People's Truth And The Brand's Truth

Intention is the new authenticity

We are living in a sort of 'Era of the Truth' in a hyper-connected and increasingly transparent society. Where truth, conflicts and differences amongst individuals rise to the surface with more intensity; where nuances become evident and human differences have a voice and meaning of their own. What used to be peripheral is becoming mainstream, affecting and touching people like never before; what's false and arrogant emerge and what's true and honest come to light.

The audiences identify what's wrong from the brand's intention, realising with ease if the brand is bluffing, making promises or even being opportunistic.

A brand narrative with a broad meaning to society materialises with the encounter between brand's purpose and human need. When the brand's truth is in tune with people's truth through relevant and meaningful stories, it creates value and takes the relationship between brands and audiences to another level.

Therefore, brands should choose the path of meaningful narratives, where stories that are based on truth and made for real people have proven to work very well. A choice that is directly related to the brand's purpose, its vocation and role in the world and to what is relevant and makes sense to the audience, like the compelling 48-minute fiction story *Córazon*[1] (a film based on a real-life patient story, told beautifully by the Montefiore Health System), also GE brand turning science into science fiction by creating their second successful podcast *Life After*[2], the documentary *The Unseen Ocean*[3], another moving story from the series 'Human made stories' by Volvo. And I am very honoured to be a part of the team for the new series *TogetHER, The Vibrant Power Around Us*[4], created and produced by our collective ASAS.br.com for Instagram global (@instagramforbusiness). This series is about how the community's power helps entrepreneurial women to not give up on their business dreams. In partnership with Instagram, we brought to life a series about women entrepreneurs whose business contributes to regenerative culture and social impact. The TogetHER series highlights the stories of a three inspiring women from the United States and Brazil who bring up two fundamental points for today's challenging world - the strength of the collective and the resilience for such uncertain times.

---

1 https://www.doingmoremontefiore.org/corazonfilm
2 https://podcasts.apple.com/gb/podcast/lifeafter-the-message/id1045990056
3 https://www.youtube.com/watch?v=mQQN2z7uZFQ
4 https://www.asas.br.com/together-ing

PATRICIA WEISS
Brand Storytelling And Branded Content: The Powerful Meeting Between People's Truth And The Brand's Truth

The protagonists of the first three episodes are: the Nigerian Simi Adebajo[5] who opened her ethnic restaurant in San Francisco, USA, which was devastated by a fire, Lovern J. Gordon[6] who started a foundation in Avon, USA, that supports women victims of domestic violence and Ketty Valencio[7] who owns a bookstore in São Paulo, Brazil, exclusively dedicated to black women writers.

All meaningful, relevant and true human stories, about people, not about the brands.

And how can brands - who want to amplify their message and value - discover the truth in people? Here is a good tip.

The Uruguayan writer Eduardo Galeano once said that what moved him to write was (in free translation):

> *"Being able to look at what is not supposed to be seen but deserves to be seen, the small, the tiny things of unknown people, the micro-world where the true greatness of the universe lives and, at the same time, to be able to contemplate the universe through a keyhole, that is, from little things, to be able to look beyond, to the great mysteries of life."*

Patricia Weiss is Head of Branded Entertainment & Content, Strategic Consultant of Brand Storytelling, Brand Purpose & Culture at the international collective ASAS.br.com. She was Creator and Curator of the first Branded Content and Brand Storytelling Post Graduation in Brazil, at Senac University. With 34-years experience in the Marketing and Advertising business, she has worked on the Marketing side at McDonald's and Citibank, at Advertising agencies Ogilvy, DM9DDB, McCann Erickson, Co-founded M&C Saatchi agency in Brazil, and Leo Burnett as the SVP Head of Planning & Integrated Experiences Latin America. Patricia was also Head of Branded Content at Abril Group. She has been a judge for Cannes Lions, CLIO Awards, Brand Film Awards NYC, The Drum Content Awards, Lisbon Ad Festival, FIAP Festival, A-List Hollywood Awards, Dubai Lynx, Cristal Festival and also a member of their Branded Entertainment Academy and speaker, at BE Awards in Australia for two years, The Gerety Awards, Festival of Media Miami and Effie Awards. Patrícia Weiss is the Chairwoman of BCMA Brazil and BCMA Portugal and a member of the BCMA Global Council.

---

5 https://vimeo.com/474251175
6 https://vimeo.com/503204476
7 https://vimeo.com/483792579

JAMES HAYR
Brand Building Content

I've always been slightly amused that the word we use to recognise someone's encounter with a digital advertisement online is called an impression. A sense or feeling about something or someone often without conscious thought or based on little evidence. You only get one chance to make a [good] first impression and click-through rates online suggest digital ads still have significant room for improvement.

If you're looking to build a brand it's the trusted channels like TV and Cinema that still get called out by industry leaders as the 'go-to' platforms. Interestingly, advertising is moving its focus away from exposure and reach to recognition and engagement - The Attention Economy. In the 'old world' it was a bit like saying you've been in touch with someone because you've sent them an email.

So, what's the implication of this for branded content? Research continues to support the fact that storytelling is an extremely powerful way for brands to make a positive impression on its customers, often communicating not just what they do, but what they stand for. At the same time consumers, increasingly, expect brands to stand for something, to have a purpose in the world, so the door is very much ajar for the advertising world to take full advantage.

The online world, not unexpectedly, was quickest to respond to the opportunity. Unfortunately, not a lot of it memorable and most destined for digital landfill. But the 'brand building' platforms like linear TV and Cinema are now also reacting which means advertisers have a chance to connect with their audiences here beyond just straightforward advertising copy with content that's thought-provoking, entertaining, memorable and, therefore, highly effective.

Channel 4 brought back home-improvement programme *Changing Rooms* in a deal that was brokered through global media agency, Mediacom for its client Dulux. Endemol Shine Group, producer of the original series, were re-engaged to create a more modern version of the programme and within months Laurence Llewelyn-Bowen was back on our screens in all his multi-coloured splendour.

JAMES HAYR
Brand Building Content

Dulux were able to exploit their association beyond the tv screen allowing the agency to create a fully rounded marketing campaign off the back of a genuinely authentic television partnership.

Did it work? Series two has just been signed off so it seems all parties are more than satisfied with how it performed. A win for the brand, Channel 4's commissioners and, most importantly, the viewer.

Sky also reacted to the opportunity. In May last year it broadcast a brand-funded one-hour mental health documentary, *Big Boys Don't Cry* featuring England rugby star Joe Marler. Brokered through Publicis owned entity, APEX Exchange and funded by Royal London it gave the brand a chance to communicate its support of positive mental health beyond using just straight advertising. Huge column inches of earned media were generated on the back of the documentary's powerful content allowing the story to live way beyond its original screen. And people still remember it.

Even the biggest screen is now getting in on the act. This year Digital Cinema Media (DCM) launched DCM Studios Presents which gives brands the opportunity to run 3–4-minute short films immediately before the trailers. Shot by their specialist film-making roster it allows brands to utilise full cinematic production effects and Dolby Atmos sound to connect with fully engaged cinema audiences on the wide screen.

Research by the neuroscience department at University College London (UCL), has proved that story-based messaging on the cinema screen is disproportionately effective in engaging the brain through several factors such as screen size, lack of distractions, being in an unfamiliar setting and communal viewing. Directors have always said their films should be viewed on the 'big screen' for audiences to get the maximum impact of their work, this now equally applies to brand stories too it would seem.

Brands also talk about 'being in culture'. They feel the need to be nimble and to react to events that happen around them in real time. Platforms like Tik Tok have both driven this phenomenon and then cleverly benefited from it commercially. Brands, therefore, feel the need to be 'always on' and an ad made 18-months ago can sometimes look a little obsolete amongst our fast-paced culture. Businesses like Paddy Power and KFC have shown what clever work can be made if you can create content that reflects cultural, societal, and even political events as they happen.

JAMES HAYR
Brand Building Content

As a result, new creators have entered the market including the likes of Influencers and even the general public.

But there is a challenge for brands here. The key to keeping innovation focused and purposeful involves finding the right balance between agility and strategy. Marketers need their agencies to provide timely insights and a speedier route to acting upon them, but they also need those insights to be coherent and focused on a clear end-goal. Brands need to find a subject, topic, or pillar to align with for the long-haul and then show how their association is affecting it for the better.

Short-termism around subjects like sustainability leaves a brand open to dangerous and potentially P&L-damaging consumer claims of 'Greenwashing'. Brand purpose needs to have an actual purpose, otherwise it serves little purpose. So, the good news for agencies and their clients is that the big brand-building platforms like TV and Cinema are now firmly in the branded content game. They have at their disposal expert creatives and directors who are comfortable making content for the wide screen but who won't turn stuff around with a 48-hour brief response deadline and 4-week production schedule. Brands still need to be in the moment but must have a long-term view of what they want their story to be and how they want consumers to think about them.

By making a memorable first impression on the wider screen, logic suggests that the impressions that follow it, wherever they appear, may need to work less hard and you may well need fewer of them to land your point. A reminder rather than a re-enforcer. All of this points to the fact that we are in a 'golden era' of media planning.

An era where the proliferation of channels requires brands and their media agencies to think about the creative and messaging that gets the best out of them. Creative that is now in many more hands than just the Creative Agency's. Creative that now requires an interdependence of thinking, not an independence of thought.

James Hayr is Co-Founder of Brand Directors and was previously Head of Global Commercial Sales for TV production powerhouse, Endemol Shine. He has led several the UK's most successful branded content departments at companies such as Verizon Media, Microsoft, Hearst, Bauer and Conde Nast. He has collaborated with some of the world's biggest brands including Coca-Cola, Ford, Shell and Chanel and has won a number of Campaign, Media Week and Cannes Lions Awards for his work.

SANDRA LEHNER
The Future Of Luxury Is Web3

Luxury brands have traditionally feared technology would erode their brand, their exclusivity as well as their unique connection with their customers. However, Web3 promises all of that and luxury brand leaders already see it as a new way to expand their brand and connect with younger audiences, while keeping the exclusivity and advancing their direct-to-customer relationships. Although many luxury brands have already embraced these new digital worlds, one has been at the forefront when it comes to Web3[1] and the metaverse[2].

Three Luxury Brands Dominating Web3

Despite Gucci being a century-old fashion company, this Italian high-end luxury fashion house based in Florence, has captured the attention of every 16-to-35-year-old over the last few years. Gucci is the top luxury brand that Gen Z and Millennials desire to wear. According to François-Henri Pinault, CEO of Kering, Gucci's parent company, Millennials and Gen Z account for nearly 50% of Gucci's total sales. Vogue has also claimed that Gucci is the most recognized brand among Gen Z consumers on TikTok. This proves that the Italian fashion brand is always an early adopter into new trends and a force to be reckoned with throughout all generations and demographics. Gucci was one of the first luxury brands to offer experiences in the digital world with video game collaborations, the digital, two-week event version of its Gucci Garden on Roblox, and its partnership with Zepeto which allowed people to buy Gucci pieces to dress their avatars. They have also been dropping multiple NFT collections, blurring the lines between digital and physical, entering the metaverse by buying a plot of digital land in The Sandbox[3] - a virtual world on the ethereum blockchain - as well as launching 'Gucci Town' - its permanent town inside of Roblox[4].

"Gucci is always looking to embrace new technologies when they can provide an enhanced experience for our customers."
Marco Bizzarri, Gucci president and CEO

---

1 Web3 is an idea for a new iteration of the World Wide Web which incorporates concepts such as decentralisation, blockchain technologies, and token-based economics
2 The metaverse is a hypothetical iteration of the Internet as a single, universal, and immersive virtual world
3 https://opensea.io/collection/superplastic-supergucci
4 https://vault.gucci.com/en-US/story/metaverse

SANDRA LEHNER
The Future Of Luxury Is Web3

> *"Now that we are able to integrate cryptocurrencies[5] within our payment system, it is a natural evolution for those customers who would like to have this option available to them."*
> **Marco Bizzarri, Gucci president and CEO**

Another luxury brand that has been very active in Web3 is Louis Vuitton.

To celebrate their 200th birthday, French fashion house Louis Vuitton (LV) dropped an epic mobile game called Louis the Game. The game has been compared to Nintendo's hit game The Legend of Zelda, but with a twist: the game explores the journey of the fashion house's mascot Vivienne. As the brand's in-game virtual avatar, Vivienne is on a mission to complete several quests, as she makes her way through the long history of Louis Vuitton's top notch craftsmanship, design and legacy while players learn about the brand and collect NFTs along the way.

The game features 30 NFTs made in collaboration with NFT artist Beeple. Beeple is the digital artist who made art history when he sold an NFT for $69 million through a first-of-its-kind auction at Christie's in 2021. The sale positioned him "among the top three most valuable living artists", according to the auction house, and brought NFTs at the forefront[6].

But how can you showcase your Louis Vuitton x Beeple NFT?

LVMH-owned Swiss luxury watchmaker Tag Heuer has the right product for you. The Tag Heuer Connected Calibre E4 smartwatch added a new functionality where users can securely connect to crypto wallets such as Metamask or Ledger Live. The watch face has three ways to display time while showcasing NFT artworks, operating with all the collections on Ethereum.

Tag Heuer CEO Frédéric Arnault believes that an NFT display will be an attractive add-on for watch owners. *"Not launching our own NFT collection but allowing collectors to use their NFTs in a new way was the most obvious first step. We speak to all passionate collectors,"* he said.

As we have seen, luxury brands are already extremely active in this space and here are the top reasons why.

---

5 https://www.voguebusiness.com/technology/gucci-takes-the-leap-will-accept-crypto-in-us-stores
6 https://www.theverge.com/2021/3/11/22325054/beeple-christies-nft-sale-cost-everydays-69-million

SANDRA LEHNER
The Future Of Luxury Is Web3

Top Five Reasons Why Luxury Brands Are at the Forefront of Web3

1. Connecting To Younger Consumers

First, to reach Gen Z and Millennials where they are. Reaching younger consumers is an investment in the future and it makes sense for luxury brands to build lasting connections through the metaverse and Web3, because that's where Millennials, Gen Z and also Gen Alpha are. As they ascend to their full earning potential, these relationships will prove very valuable, both inside and outside the metaverse.

2. Providing Exclusive Digital Experiences Not Possible IRL

Web3 enables luxury brands to offer their most devoted consumers experiences that simply would not be possible in the real world, like the *Louis the Game*, for example. It also offers young fans, who do not have the purchasing power yet, to buy a piece of their favorite brand in the digital world. Virtual sneakers from brands like Gucci have already proved wildly popular, with a price point of $17.99.

3. Generating Scarcity

While selling skins for digital avatars means reaching a broader audience, NFTs are also a new way for luxury brands to create scarcity – a cornerstone of their brand promise. There are a limited number of Bored Apes, Pudgy Penguins, and Crypto Punks out there. These two markets were made for each other, what collaborations such as the Crypto Punks x Tiffany's collection prove. When paired with exclusive luxury items, NFT's can only increase their perceived scarcity and value.

4. Ensuring Authenticity

Since blockchain technology offers a precise record of an items' origin and sales history, Web3 provides luxury brands the possibility to track ownership, ensure authenticity, and maintain their exclusivity. The Aura Blockchain Consortium[7], the world's first global luxury blockchain, takes certification a step further, though. Its founding members include LVMH, Prada Group, Cartier, and Mercedes-Benz and their objective is to provide consumers with a high level of transparency and traceability throughout the lifecycle of a product.

7 https://www.lvmh.com/news-documents/news/lvmh-partners-with-other-major-luxury-companies-on-aura-the-first-global-luxury-blockchain/

5. Creating A New Haute Couture

Haute Couture has always been a central component of luxury fashion. Vogue once described Haute Couture pieces as 'walking pieces of art'. Au contraire to Prêt-a-Porter fashion (=ready to wear), Haute Couture pieces are designed to be worn by a few clients, if not only one. They are usually only seen on runways, museums, and exclusive events – not on the streets. But in the metaverse anything is possible, and Gen-Z views the metaverse as a safe place to freely express themselves and experiment with identities. Here clothes can be as eccentric and avant-garde as the designers and users want them to be[8].

3 Steps to a Web3 Strategy

As promising as all of this sounds, luxury brands must make sure Web3 fits into their brand strategy and their Web3 ventures have purpose and a value proposition.

1. Clear Consumer-Centric Value Proposition

Just launching a metaverse-related project out of FOMO is one of the biggest mistakes many luxury brands make right now. Simple NFT drops without utility are seen as 'cash-grabs' and can affect your brand sentiment negatively.

2. Long-Term Strategy

Utility has a lot to do with long-term thinking. Make sure creating a community in Web3 fits your brand's long-term strategy and identity.

3. Follow Your Audience

The target audience must always be the North Star. Go where your audience already is, instead of launching your own platform. But it is important that your brand fits into the environment of the platform and gives the users actual value.

As we have seen, the most obvious way fashion brands can show up in Web3 is by selling their products as digital wearables via NFTs in virtual worlds like Decentraland, Roblox, and Fortnite.

---

[8] https://www.businesswire.com/news/home/20220419005232/en/Razorfish-Study-Finds-52-of-Gen-Z-Gamers-Feel-More-Like-Themselves-in-the-Metaverse-than-in-Real-Life

SANDRA LEHNER
The Future Of Luxury Is Web3

Digital wearables can be introduced on social media and tried on via personalised avatars before physical clothes are even produced - and this is another interesting aspect of Web3. The Aura Blockchain Consortium example showed that the traceability throughout the lifecycle of a product has huge benefits for clothing brands in terms of supply chain management and research in the future. That's why I believe Web3 will be the future of fashion. Not just for luxury fashion, but also in terms of making fast fashion sustainable.

Sandra Lehner is a Creative Strategy Director & International Speaker, specialising on connecting TV and Digital content to reach the Gen-Z audience. In 2018, she won the Swiss Marketing Award 'Thought Leader of the Year' for her work in the Branded Entertainment sector and with Gen-Z. Sandra is experienced in developing Branded Entertainment formats. She has over 10 years experience in social media storytelling and strategy with a focus on the Gen-Z audience. She has worked with brands, networks, production companies, and agencies on creative strategies, interactive storytelling, and brand integrations. She speaks at international conferences. Sandra is a BCMA Global Advisor.

MARTIN LAING
Converging Storylines

How 20 years of technological innovation and adoption changed branded content

The technological evolution of the filmmaking tools at hand, have brought us all closer, converging and blurring the lines between genres, sectors, and disciplines.

CNN Create, the global in-house studio for CNN International Commercial, has expanded its production techniques to now offer CNN's clients' video content that uses the same technology pioneered in blockbusters such as *The Batman, The Mandalorian* and *House of The Dragon*.

As the studio's Director of Production & Global Executive Producer, a key focus for me is to keep innovating - to find new ways to tell stories. The next focus for our offering is driven by a commitment to devise bold content that's also sustainable. Using Virtual Production, the incredible LED wall screen, and Unreal Engine gaming software pioneered by Hollywood level productions, we're able to programme any location scenario into the volume stage, from anywhere, on, or off this world, whilst never having to be more than a few miles from our office.

This approach also offers up an opportunity to further reduce the carbon emissions associated with production travel, and 'boots-on-the-ground' live action filming. This links with our recently launched Create Responsibly initiative, that aims to support our industry's goal to achieve net zero by 2030.

As a member of the Advertising Associations Ad Net Zero steering group, we now run every live action film through the AdGreen carbon calculator to measure, reduce and offset the carbon footprint of production. The future certainly looks framed by new technology like Virtual Production, and the cultural, and professional 'Climate Change' rallying point. Having the bandwidth and opportunity to refine the way we produce branded content like this has taken the majority of my career in the sector.

MARTIN LAING
Converging Storylines

Twenty years ago, as I was entering the industry proper, it still felt clearly segmented. You had to choose clear routes, even though I, like so many of my peers had grown up in the 90s with a DIY attitude to filmmaking. This approach had always been around since Super8 cameras, but suddenly in the 90s home camcorders were attainable by more households than ever before. I started directing short films, persuading friends to feature in them, all self-shot on hi-8 video, with basic linear edit equipment. It quickly shifted to building a pc edit suite via mail order, playing with open source edit software, being wowed by the idea of a 10 GB hard-drive, and read-write speeds supported by firewire 400. Saving every bit of pocket-money and part-time job earnings, using up a Christmas and Birthday cash to buy a mini DV video camera to start creating 'professionally'.

MTV in those days felt like a guiding light of 'gonzo' video production, Spike Jonze self-shooting on Sony PD150s, the explosion of reality-TV spurred on by the ground-breaking *The Real World*. The idea of what was considered 'professional' had changed. In the same way Paul McCartney's self-titled debut solo album birthed the idea of 'Indi' self-produced music in the early 70s, ultimately because the recording studio technology had miniaturised, and could be set-up in a spare room. With distribution eventually being democratised and put into the hands of the creators. The same happened with video, suddenly camera and editing kit was accessible, and once digital platforms like YouTube appeared we had the opportunity to create and distribute ourselves. The MTV kids had taken over and re-shaped the industry along the way. Access to technology and information gave my generation a different point of view. I would argue more so than my parents and grandparents' generation, or maybe it felt accelerated because we bridged the 'analogue to digital' gap. By the time we managed to have a go at building careers, our attitude to what was possible and considered 'professional' had changed forever. My fascination with anything George Lucas touched inspired me and so many others to believe that anything is possible. The feedback Mr Lucas would give to his team at Industrial Light & Magic (ILM) when a concept couldn't be realised was to 'Try Harder'. The ideas in his head seemed to outpace where technology was in the moment, forcing innovation.

As we know, with hindsight, the 'noughties' proved to be a huge period of change, with advancing camera and computer hardware, and software updates that felt like huge leaps back then, rather than incremental improvements. The Mini DV days of the late 90s had quickly shifted into 720p and solid-state HD video.

MARTIN LAING
Converging Storylines

Seeing the *Phantom Menace* for the first time knowing it was shot on digital cameras, the first of its kind at such grand scale, was a strange and exciting moment. The slow death of film had begun, along with the convergence of the myriad of sectors within the world of moving image.

When I graduated from film school, I had dreams of moving to London - to Soho specifically - to start a creative trajectory through the mill of junior roles, with aspirations of becoming a successful producer in a production company or ad-agency, making commercials and music videos, maybe even eventually finding my feet somewhere in the feature-length documentary and fiction feature film world. This was the obvious path all my film school peers also aspired to at the time. What I hadn't expected is where I found myself, working at the number one news organisation on the planet, in a niche corner of the advertising sector making branded content films all over the world. Although, my parents did meet whilst working at The Scotsman newspaper in Edinburgh in the 70's. Deep down, the idea of working for a news organisation seemed to make sense to me.

Landing a job at CNN in the newly created commercials department started as a way into Soho, at our old offices on Great Marlborough Street. In those early days we didn't use the term 'native advertising' or branded content. We made SFCF's (Short Form Commercial Films) or Commercial Vignettes, nobody really knew what we meant until they saw the film. Short branded documentaries filmed on small, fixed lens digital video cameras with real people, no actors. It felt like we were on the outskirts of the industry, trying to explain what we did at Soho industry parties felt like falling into a trap. I didn't feel much respect coming our way, back then. Not many people seemed to be doing it. Oh, how things have changed.

Every time I thought about the next move to the wider world of production, the branded content horizon seemed to expand further with a new opportunity to create content for an international client. The pages in my old passport are a good reminder of how truly global my journey has been. The opportunities to explore new forms of branded content have kept me wanting more ever since.

Brands now command trust with audiences as storytellers in their own right. No different from a movie studio or film director with a reputable body of work. Brands have stories to tell, and with studios like CNN Create, have captured storytelling opportunities in branded content that didn't exist in other parts of the industry.

MARTIN LAING
Converging Storylines

After decades of brand integration in mainstream media audiences are incredibly sophisticated and desensitized to brand inclusion if product integration is achieved organically. Coca Cola having featured in films since King Kong in 1933 acquired Columbia Pictures in the year I was born! shuttering in an accelerated era of Coke can product placement in hit movies like Ghostbusters and ET. But back then the studio brand that audiences found trust in were Columbia and Tri Star. The titles didn't begin with 'Coca Cola Films Present'. Fast forward to today, and we are excitedly waiting for our go to shopping app or technology brand to keep us entertained and informed with the next film or episode streaming release.

We are also used to seeing product disclaimers at the start of dramas like *The Morning Show* or travel doc series *The Long Way Up*. Audiences want authentic stories, we hold trust and meaning in brands across all parts of our lives. Through brand ambassadors this trust is heightened further. I know this first hand, for so many reasons linked to my childhood growing up in the east coast of Scotland obsessed with Star Wars, knowing my grandfather as a paratrooper and motorbike dispatch rider during WW2, and being swept up in the Trainspotting frenzy as a teenager during 'Cool Britannia' has created a scenario that anything Ewan McGregor seems to put his name to speaks directly to me, (Star Wars, Motorbikes, Belstaff and VW Buzz) becoming a focus of aspiration whether I like it or not.

The growth seen in documentaries with the support of all the streamers has helped our form of human centric branded content. Audiences are watching as many documentaries as they are feature film and dramas[1]. The recent success of the Oscar winning WeTransfer branded film by Riz Ahmed, *The Long Goodbye* simply shows an acceptance that someone has to pay for the content. Over the past 20-years we have seen the respect and power of the branded content genre grow exponentially.

Ideas by passionate and driven people has forced technological advancement generating content trend flourishes. As social content platforms have launched, evolved and folded, aspect ratios have expanded, and squeezed, and expanded again to a limitless landscape of experiential immersive virtual and augmented reality. The reshaping of how, why, and when we consume video content continues to evolve rapidly.

---

1 https://www.hollywoodreporter.com/movies/movie-features/documentary-streaming-age-filmmaker-debate-ethics-payments-1235221541/

MARTIN LAING
Converging Storylines

The Camera and editing technology have developed so far that the lines have blurred between what's considered amateur, 'prosumer', professional, Social, TV, Documentary, Immersive, Advert or Feature Film.

As professionals across the sectors, we all now find ourselves using the same camera and editing technology, with all the camera chip K's we will ever need, and terabytes supported by terabytes of storage. It's the skill and talent of the individual creative or creative teams which is laid bare that will shine through.

On the other hand, the form of smart phone produced, and distributed content has changed what audiences accept and respond to. For some, video content is only viewed on their smart phones, never mind laptop, 4k TV or in the Cinema. Social content, with a shelf-life of as many seconds as it takes to watch it created a form of 'throw-away' content that may have affected attention spans and expectations.

The fragmentation of audiences, groups, tribes, geos through platforms, targeting, algorithms, and endless consumer choice gives storytellers so many areas to play, share and speak to. Personalised content is still tailored to individual consumers based on data collected about them. Are we now all destined to be trapped inside our own content echo chambers? Are these echo chambers already beginning to materialise as a tangible place within the Metaverse? As tribes begin waging virtual ideological warfare in the Metaverse from their living rooms, we will need to remind ourselves to experience the new, listen to all sides in order to grow and learn.

Immersive, world building storytelling opportunities that has existed in Gaming, now transpose into VR and the Metaverse. The convergence of this technology with human centric branded content is a fascinating future. I could get used to the idea of plugging in to another person's world from time to time, to have a walk through their life, to explore their perspective. Knowing all the time and upfront that the person's real-life story was told and visualised with the support of a brand. That's ok with me.

When I speak to creatives, many have experience in writing, directing, producing, filming, and editing. Some even influencers, with experience across all sectors. It seems clearer now than ever, with the freedom granted to us by technological innovation and adoption, that we are simply and proudly all storytellers.

MARTIN LAING
Converging Storylines

Our individual style, vision, and perseverance to deliver, is all that stands in the way of captivating audiences with extraordinary branded content.

Martin Laing is the Director of Production & Global Executive Producer of Create Brand Studio at CNN International Commercial. He is an experienced and Executive Producer who has built and managed creative production teams from the ground up. Martin is a creative leader with a proven track record of delivering quality, award-winning and engaging content for every medium. During his extensive career he has overseen multi-million pound production budgets and managed international crews, remotely and onset. He has developed content strategy and Exec Produced, Produced and Directed hundreds of multi-platform projects working directly with with some of the world's largest brands.

TOM HIGGINS
How Gifting Became An Inflection Point For Brand Storytelling

Giving and receiving gifts plays an important role in our social fabric and the practice has existed since the beginning of human civilisation. While gift giving may feel like second nature, the psychology behind the gift we choose and how we present it says a lot about how we build and maintain bonds.

Due to the emotional connection that gifting fosters, it can also be used as a powerful storytelling tool. By tapping into the power of influence, companies can use gifting to their advantage to grow brand love by creating a deeper connection with a product or service.

In this respect, gifting has become an inflection point for brand storytelling in earned media as it can simultaneously support both PR and marketing efforts. For the former, it helps boost positive word of mouth, which is essential to boost a brand's reputation, while for the latter it can be a direct sales driver. In bringing the two together, gifting occupies a unique space in the influencer marketing mix that has proven results.

Prioritise meaningful relationships above all

Influencer marketing will only work if you connect storytellers with the brands, products, and services you know they – and their audiences – will love, and no algorithm can beat good old-fashioned legwork. Just like choosing a present for a loved one, creating a thoughtful, personal gift is a lot more meaningful and will result in an evocative connection.

It is paramount to carry out due diligence to carefully curate such relationships – only then will a positive, long-lasting relationship between a brand and content creator be established. Look carefully at the audience, content feed and engagement of each influencer to ensure you are creating a good match, or risk earned media content looking inauthentic, or even worse, forced.

For example, in a recent campaign for Gosh! Food, we micro-targeted influencers with interests aligned to the brand's product offer.

TOM HIGGINS
How Gifting Became An Inflection Point For Brand Storytelling

This included vegan and vegetarian creators, health and fitness creators and foodies. We then only sent gifted products to influencers that wanted to try them. This was a fantastic way to boost conversion, which was more than 85%.

This can also lead to long-lasting relationships. Brands are using Gifta to discover influencers for paid opportunities, and in turn, influencers are using Gifta to be discovered by brands. This symbiotic relationship ensures both parties can build a genuine relationship built on a shared love for the product or service.

Effective campaigns don't need to drain your budgets, but a small investment can go a long way

Running an influencer campaign can be expensive. With some macro-influencers charging upwards of five figures per social media post, businesses are being priced out of the market. But influencer marketing needn't be expensive. Gifting is just one way that brands can meaningfully connect with online opinion formers and generate high-quality earned media, without breaking the bank.

One way for brands to do this is to look to micro and nano influencers. These creators have a niche and fiercely loyal communities that enable brands to tap into relevant sub-cultures that are more likely to act if they are recommended a brand or product.

While their follower numbers might not be the largest, they often have much higher engagement rates which increase their selling power. Because of this, trend-watchers have predicted that micro and nano influencers will continue to grow in importance over this year and next.

Something we suggest to our clients at Gifta is to amplify assets by purchasing content usage rights from the influencer after a campaign has ended. For a relatively small investment, companies can use this content across their marketing channels such as paid social, website and out-of-home.

This not only helps save on expensive photo and video shoots, but ads based on user generated content receive four times higher click-through rates and a 50% drop, in cost-per-click compared to average ads. It's win, win.

TOM HIGGINS
How Gifting Became An Inflection Point For Brand Storytelling

Creative freedom builds positive PR

Unlike paid campaigns, where influencers are under a contractual obligation to promote a product or service, gifting gives influencers the freedom to retain full editorial control.

This means that influencers feel empowered to leave honest reviews, can decide not to write about a product, or can write about a product in their own words – free of jargon and marketing speak. As a result, audiences view these earned media posts as more authentic and so engagement rates are naturally higher.

Releasing control over messaging can make some companies and brands nervous. However, we do offer creators a helping hand by providing an information card, which includes key facts about the products we have gifted. This ensures influencers have everything they need for creating their social media content. This ensures key brand messages are subtly woven into content in a way that feels 100% authentic.

Measurement can help demonstrate positive ROI

No campaign is worth doing if you can't measure the results correctly. At Gifta, influencers give us permission to track their Instagram data which enables us to report in real-time on granular metrics using our proprietary measurement platform.

For any influencer gifting campaign, metrics including impressions, engagement rate, type and frequency of content, number of key messages and feedback should be benchmarked and measured to enable you to effectively calculate return on investment.

Tom Higgins is the Co-Founder of Gifta, the UK's first brand-to-influencer gifting logistics company. They connect storytellers with brands they truly love, producing only 100% authentic content. Prior to Gifta, Tom enjoyed a career in sales and marketing for over a decade, but he realised that the nine-to-five roles really weren't working for him so decided to travel and find a way he did want to work. He saw that while the founding team had a variety of skills and tools, the most useful was some of the most commonly found online business applications, like Google Business Suite, Canva and Xero.

DR TAUHEED A. RAMJAUN
Fighting Branded Misinformation

With great power comes great responsibility says the old adage. Many brands are now being involved in the publishing of informative content that employ journalistic modes of production but without the gatekeeping mechanisms that would exist within a traditional news organisation. While this can be seen as a major advantage for brands, there is also a need for branded content practitioners to consider the potential negative consequences that branded misinformation could have on consumer well-being and society at large.

For the purpose of this essay, I will focus on the notion of 'misinformation' which has been defined in UNESCO's Handbook for Journalism Education and Training as: "information that is false, but the person who is disseminating it believes that it is true."[1] In the context of branded content practice, this could for example involve a content creator (e.g., a health and fitness influencer) developing informational content commissioned by a brand based on inaccurate, partial, or misleading facts that both the influencer and the brand manager believe to be true. They might be presented with some pseudo-scientific research findings that could be part of a grander scheme of advancing a certain ideology by a particular group. By disseminating such informational content through their own communication channels (or those that they endorse), brands not only become vectors of misinformation but contribute to amplifying the reach.

Brands tend to sometimes portray themselves as victims of misinformation and the conservations within the marketing sphere have tended to be more slanted towards brand safety, brand protection or brand trust. However, the growing involvement of brands in the endorsement, production, or dissemination of various forms of informational content, they also need to seriously reflect upon the overall impact of their practices on consumer well-being and on society at large. They need to start thinking about the contribution of certain forms of 'branded misinformation' in the overall pollution of the information landscape and the profound consequences in the long-term.

[1] C. Wardle & H. Derakhshan, 'Thinking about 'information disorder': formats of misinformation, disinformation, and mal-information', in C. Ireton & J. Posetti (eds.), Journalism, 'Fake News' & Disinformation: Handbook for Journalism Education and Training, (UNESCO, Paris: 2018), 44-55: 44

DR TAUHEED A. RAMJAUN
Fighting Branded Misinformation

The publication of this book marks an important milestone for the branded content community, and I believe it is a good time for practitioners to reflect upon how they can work together to fight branded misinformation in their everyday practice. I propose below some suggestions that could initiate some steps in that direction:

- Brands need to consider slowing down the pace of branded content creation. As Professor of Marketing Mark Peterson puts it, brands need rather work on building the capacity of in-house staff involved in supporting the brand so that they are better equipped to fight fake news in "an era characterised by volatility, uncertainty, complexity and ambiguity (VUCA)"[2]

- Brands need to encourage staff involved with informational content creation to spend more cognitive efforts in analysing the sources of information. Brand management need to take serious steps in encouraging a source verification methodology that is systematically carried out by in-house or outsourced content creators to ensure more reliability in the information creation process

- Branded content creators (especially the ill-experienced social media influencers) involved in the development of informational content could get more formal training in helping them understand and navigate issues associated with misinformation and information disorder. There are also various free resources and tools available online that could prove useful (some examples are provided in the table overleaf)

Branded content creators are becoming more powerful and resourceful players in the information space, especially those involved with social media platforms. While many are constantly striving towards enhancing their storytelling and audience engagement skills, they could also think about levelling up their misinformation fighting skills.

I am aware that the issue of misinformation in our contemporary society is a complex one and that there is no easy or quick-fix solution.

---

2 M. Peterson, 'A high-speed world with fake news: Brand managers take warning', *Journal of Product and Brand Management*, 29, 2 (2020), 234-245:234

DR TAUHEED A. RAMJAUN
Fighting Branded Misinformation

However, a starting point might be for brands and their content creators to realise that they are also part of the problem and not always think of themselves as the victims of misinformation.

Resource	Institution	Description from Authors	URL
IMVAIN	Stony Brook Center for News Literacy	A methodological approach to evaluate sources who show up in news stories.	https://digitalresource.center/content/introducing-imvain
Google Fact Check Tools	Google in collaboration with independent fact-checking partners	The Fact Check Tools consist of two tools: Fact Check Explorer and Fact Check Markup Tool. Both tools aim to facilitate the work of fact checkers, journalists, and researchers.	https://toolbox.google.com/factcheck/explorer
The 'top ten' multi-stakeholder media literacy resources for resilience to information disorder	Bournemouth University Centre for Excellence in Media Practice	A list of useful resources that were rated highly by the research participant groups (students, teachers, librarians and journalists).	http://mlfn.cemp.ac.uk/toolkit/
Humanising Public Health: A Public Guide to Best Practice	Bournemouth University Science, Health & Data Communication Research Group	A best practice guide for comic artists and science communicators who want to craft public health messages.	https://www.covidcomics.org/ahrc-project/best-practice-guidelines/

Dr Tauheed Ramjaun is a Senior Lecturer in Corporate and Marketing Communications at Bournemouth University. His research interests are currently orientated around three main areas: (1) corporate brand communications (2) online brand communities (3) responsible consumption practices. Tauheed's PhD dissertation explored corporate (charity) brand relationships within a non-profit context. As a 'fused' academic, he also assists various types of organisations in solving brand-related issues through the understanding and application of relevant theoretical concepts and frameworks. Prior to joining academia, he worked for two years within the United Nations where he contributed in raising the online communications profile of the UNDP Country Office (Mauritius). He spent several years within the advertising/public relations industry holding various positions such as Client Service Executive, Strategic Planner, and Head of Advertising & creative Services.

MONIQUE CENTRONE PH.D.
Making Sense Of NFTs

NFTs (non-fungible tokens) have gained notoriety as an accessible way to buy and sell digital art. They have garnered the attention of brands across categories as a potential new line of business. But is this a real opportunity for most brands? How can and should brands and businesses be responding to this ever-shifting landscape, to tap into new opportunities and leverage growth?

In recent years, cryptocurrency has demonstrated itself as one of the defining financial trends of our time. In contrast NFTs, a form of digitally produced and blockchain based art, feels like the defining cultural trend of the past year, generating a total of $5.4 billion in profits through sales of the tokens in 2021[1]. Despite all the publicity, the space still feels like it is mostly for insiders: gamers, investors, and luxury brands.

As such, Ipsos investigated the world of NFTs. We have gone on the journey of creating (aka *minting*) an NFT. Our research shows that NFTs have opened new possibilities for brand storytelling, and that engaging NFT communities is a creative, yet more risk-averse way to help brands tap into the phenomenon and play in the space. Here we will present learnings designed to empower brands across many categories, with insights on how to innovatively engage with consumers and shape new brand narratives.

Search and social data provide a concrete basis for understanding how the wider public has been exploring NFTs. Globally, the terms 'NFT' or 'NFTs' have been mentioned a staggering 169 million times in the past twelve months, 93.6 million of which were in the past three months alone. Both search and social volumes for the past twelve months (indexed UK Google search volumes for NFTs and social mentions of 'NFTs' versus GBP Bitcoin) show interest is overall very high, demonstrating that NFTs have emphatically captured the public's attention. As the space has gained so much popularity, it would be appealing to brands to want to monetise this opportunity and start creating their own NFTs.

---

1 "Quarterly NFT Market Report" NonFungible. (2022) Q1. Palmerston, Ontario. Available here: https://nonfungible.com/reports/2022/en/q1-quarterly-nft-market-report

MONIQUE CENTRONE PH.D.
Making Sense Of NFTs

However, it is important to fully understand what they are first, to decide how brands across most categories might capitalise on the NFT space.

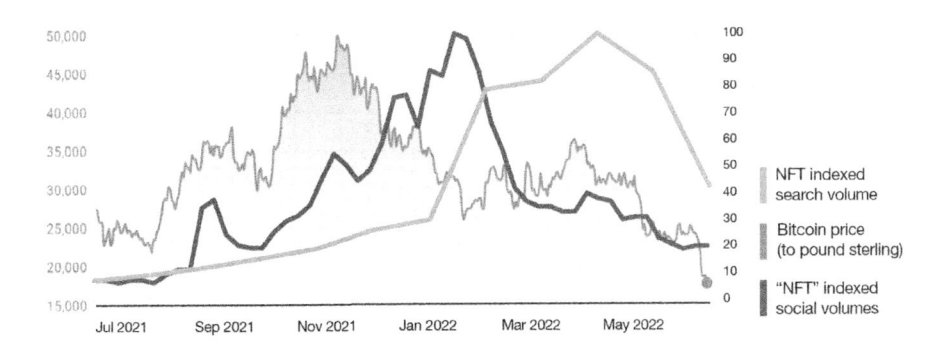

Indexed searches broadly map to the Bitcoin price, although NFTs peaked in late January – some delay after Bitcoin's November peak.

Source:
Google trends, P12M, UK
Synthesio, P12M, Worldwide

NFTs are digital assets. Whilst they are not cryptocurrencies themselves, they are supported by the same blockchain technology[2]. More simply, they are another thing to buy or invest in, usually digital art, but with a highly trackable claim to ownership. And the trackability is important because digital things like a JPG or an MP3 can be duplicated repeatedly, rendering the idea of 'ownership' meaningless.

The trackability is possible because an NFT itself is a unique digital code, creating a unique claim on it that is publicly accessible and, therefore, transparent. The hard to grasp technological nature of the blockchain should not deter us from trying to dig deeper on the myriad opportunities it might represent.

Artists, art enthusiasts, digital and cultural experts, as well as investors all have an opinion on those opportunities. Our findings show that the world of NFTs is inherently polarising. Despite many wanting to be part of the momentum, others feel there is a strong speculative dimension to this space. A recent estimate indicated that up to 90% of the market may be speculative selling[3]. Critiques range from, on the one hand, accusations not dissimilar to 'insider' trading, which can artificially elevate the cost of the art at the

---
[2] "IBM What is blockchain technology?" IBM (2022) Available here: https://www.ibm.com/uk-en/topics/what-is-blockchain
[3] "A sceptic's guide to Crypto: NFT mania" (2022) Available here: https://play.acast.com/s/ft-tech-tonic/a-sceptics-guide-to-crypto-nft-mania

release[4]; on the other hand, there is the issue of the seemingly bankrupt nature of mass-produced art based in trending investment value rather than substantive aesthetic value[5].

For the rest of us, those unfamiliar with the blockchain, neophyte investors, or brands eager to start producing their own branded NFTs - the barriers to entry feel considerable, and it would be hard to know how or where to enter the space and translate this excitement to actual economic gains. Most brands are not the kind that can sell a digital reproduction of their product, for example a designer handbag that sells for 200% the cost of the real thing in the metaverse. Take Nike as an example, that recently managed to sell 600 pairs of NFT sneakers in just six minutes, for a total of $3.1 million.

NFTs seem like the second big wave of public excitement (crypto being the first) happening because of blockchain technology. Finding new uses for the blockchain is like a grand social experiment. NFTs are part of this socio-cultural process of hammering out uses for a new technology.

As claims to ownership in digital space have seemed to nearly fall apart, the blockchain as a strong tracking technology solves the problem of digital reproducibility. Think about the phrase information wants to be free, Stewart Brand's famous aphorism, first uttered at the Hackers Conference in Marin County, California in 1984.

---

4 "NFT marketplace OpenSea valued at more than $13bn" The BBC (2022) Available here: https://www.bbc.co.uk/news/technology-59880739
5 World of Women WOW (2022) https://www.worldofwomen.art/provenance

MONIQUE CENTRONE PH.D.
Making Sense Of NFTs

It became the call of hackers and internet enthusiasts at the early phase of the internet, legitimising countless platforms that have facilitated mass pirating of protected content. It is an ethos that has worked against strong control of rights and protections, that has arguably stifled creative development since. Understanding this about NFTs helps us see that there is a good overall rationale for what NFTs do, in terms of protection of creative output, even alongside justified criticism.

While investment in NFTs may lead to financial freedom for some individuals, and growth for some brands, these opportunities are accompanied by new risks and challenges, including the hotly debated climate impact as well as an amplification of the digital divide[6]. Because of such claims, there needs to be a safer way to make something of it. And our exploration of the long journey toward *minting art* - or the process of uploading art to the blockchain which converts digital data into digital assets that cannot be changed, edited, or deleted – does give us some new ways to understand entry points for brands.

The minting process presents a compelling way to understand the value of NFTs and a more sensible way for brands to enter the cultural phenomenon of it. These fascinating communities have a quirky identity, with off-beat names like Crypto Punks, Ninja Hideout, Mutant Cat, Larva Labs, all connoting underground rebellion positioned against the monotonous normalcy endured by the rest of the world.

For NFTs, while the art itself does play some role, the specific piece you will ultimately own is not important. What is important, however, is that you will own something; but what one gets is more than just the NFT of a wonky digital ape; it is an identity as an NFT owner in a specific NFT collective, because there is a significant investment beyond money – it is time and social energy spent developing the art collective's identity.

Observations from interviews of NFT investors, and from our study of the NFT minting journey in which we spoke to artists during a minting process, shows that the piece one ultimately owns – not known at the outset - is only one aspect of the investment. For artists that seek to mint a collection, building of the NFT community of investors is paramount.

---

6 Energy of Blockchain Technologies. European Union Blockchain Observatory & Forum, Papageorgio, O. et al. (2021). Available here:
https://www.eublockchainforum.eu/sites/default/files/reports/Energy%20Efficiency%20of%20Blockchain%20Technologies_1_0.pdf

MONIQUE CENTRONE PH.D.
Making Sense Of NFTs

Equally, when looking to invest, the search for the 'right' community is too. The 'right' community is determined by a multitude of factors, which begins with the artist's past work, as well as the mission and personality of the artist, and the transparent functioning of the community, the community vibe, the excitement generated in the group and other social factors that confer desirability on the digital asset and, therefore, its ultimate economic value.

For the investor, the journey often begins with a search, which seems to happen primarily on Twitter. Twitter generated almost 90% of NFT-related posts in the past 12 months, and it is a key resource for those wishing to learn, engage and exchange views on NFTs. From there, once a potential investor has narrowed down the search for the collection they might like, the journey moves to the social chatting platform known as Discord.

Discord is a digital place where people hang out and chat together, typically while they are doing other things together, like gaming or watching online content. The platform is the equivalent of the chat room in the early 1990s, and it is where members of a specific NFT community share their excitement on their upcoming NFT collection. Potential investors must therefore not only buy into the collective: they must also align with and help build the identity of the NFT community within Discord (which is then viral-marketed back on Twitter).

Although people might certainly come to enjoy the visual aspect of the art, few join an NFT because they find the artwork itself initially beautiful. Like much of modern art, members of a community buy into it because they like what it represents, and they connect with the ethos of the artists, and the specific community.

In the context of NFT communities, the hype prior to minting is critical in developing the value of the ownership, attracting new people who want to share and celebrate their identity as an owner within that collective. Essentially, it is the sociability and energy of the of the overall collective that ultimately attracts enough members to finally mint the art.

Taken together, the community hype is a central aspect of overall investment, and it plays on one of the deepest motivations of human existence: that of belonging. Engaging the community creates new forms of social connection and gives a new way to find one's tribe in the digital sphere, a key part of what people do more generally in the digital world.

MONIQUE CENTRONE PH.D.
Making Sense Of NFTs

There are variable motivations for the different actors that engage NFT collectives: for artists, the community is market access, a somewhat more accessible and democratic art scene; for gamers, communities are an exciting space for play and exploration; crypto investors on the other hand, see them as a space of innovation and participation in the blockchain experiment.

In this way, *NFTs are generative.* Their random cultural nature, sometimes funny cultural memes (Bored Apes), other times social values and conscious driven (World of Women collective), they allow for different meanings to be given by different industries and different individuals. Overall, NFTs capture the cultural moment by the random quirkiness of the art pieces generated, but whose users choose to find something intriguing in, something to identify with or celebrate – collectively, something to believe in. The ownership of the NFT is the final prize for the excitement around their community's pieces.

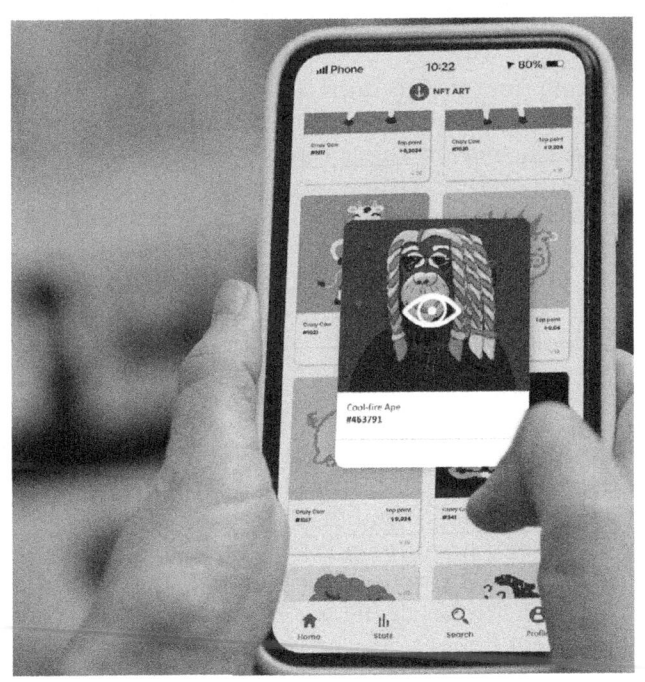

Viewed in its more social aspects, NFTs are about more than just digital investments – the cultural hook they create, the art that catches a niche group's imagination – elevates to economic value what are to outsiders seemingly non-sensical digital artworks by way of generating social value – a sense of collective belief and purpose in the ownership of the art, powered by community-based nature of NFT ownership. In a deep way, the community is king and can be considered a brand in itself.

MONIQUE CENTRONE PH.D.
Making Sense Of NFTs

We conclude that while the luxury space is now teeming with NFT opportunities, very few brands at this stage have the kinds of product that would have value in an NFT format. However, our analysis highlights different opportunities. NFTs hold the promise of a new form of brand engagement with younger generations, through partnerships with NFT communities.

The space can be considered a new way for brands to not only understand but also to engage new audiences. Brands across every category are already thinking about how to engage Generation Z, and Generation Alpha. And newer platforms like Discord and Steam, that create socialising, multitasking, and content exhibiting at the foundation of NFT communities have already become an inherent part of how this generation communicates with one another. While the price of the art may fluctuate, it is the communities that become a new pathway for brands to create engagement and interact with participatory pre-built communities created in these platforms.

Collectives aiming for social impact are an emerging phenomenon. Inclusion and diversity are critical topics of our time and there are several collectives based on this principle including Women Rise NFT, ARTXV and Moon Landing. Others support charitability around mental health (such as Blazed Cats) or families in need (Fast Food Punks). There is even a new NFT platform called Metagood, which hosts collectives with a charitable aim, and which allow portions of sales to go to donations. It seems likely at this time that social values-oriented collectives will continue to grow.

While brand activation is sometimes about highlighting inclusive values, it is much broader than that. Where NFT collectives can be understood as a new kind of brand, as we have described above, engagement and marketing through NFT collectives is about finding the collective/s or even hosting one that complements your brand personality in its core characteristics – something playful or caring, or empowering or science-vibe. It means having something metaverse-y to talk about to connect better younger generations.

While this is a very emergent space, brand partnerships are not. Reese Witherspoon's media company, Hello Sunshine, announced a storytelling partnership with the NFT community World of Women (WoW)[7], an NFT collective with a mission to 'create a beautiful, diverse, empowering collection and thriving new community'.

---

7 World of Women WOW (2022) https://www.worldofwomen.art/provenance

MONIQUE CENTRONE PH.D.
Making Sense Of NFTs

This unique collaboration gives a new marketing platform, generating educational and entertaining content for both Hello Sunshine and WoW, alongside events that celebrate representation and inclusivity. Another partnership, between the collective ARC[8] and Millennium Hotels & Resorts gives ARC members access to bespoke real-world experiences across the hospitality group's global footprint and the opportunity for digital co-creation in its latest venture, M Social Decentraland.

ARC is a diverse community that spans a variety of geographies and industries and includes influencers across fashion, cinema, and investment as well as thought leaders. They partner with brands to give members *"the opportunity to connect, play and grow in a community across Web 2 experiences and Web 3 opportunities,"* says the founder Kiat Lim. Even while brand partnerships are an embedded practice, these examples illustrate creative ways to explore, understand and utilise NFT communities and how brands might align to them.

The rise of NFTs is too important for brands to ignore. The value of NFTs is rooted in community identity. This should bring a challenge, but also, some reassurance to brands: challenge in that brands need to get creative in how they bank on new technologies and cultural phenomena, sharpening the need to listen and empathise to deliver their purpose; and reassurance in that aligning with a community is an easier path forward than jumping into minting NFTs, and that closer listening to the market has forever been the secret to success.

Monique Centrone, Ph.D. is the UK Semiotics Lead at Ipsos Advisory. She is a brand specialist and cultural analyst focused on how brands fit within cultures. As a sociologist she is trained at the highest level in quantitative and qualitative methods undertaking product R&D, consulting on innovative research design. Monique is a passionate creative thinker and problem solver - reverse engineering culture, asking the right questions to evoke the structure and meaning within any organisation, group, object/product, idea or concept and brings big ideas to bear on the strategic challenges of their clients.

---

8 'Singapore Private NFT Club ARX Teams up with Millennium' Bloomberg Tax (2022). Available here: https://news.bloombergtax.com/crypto/singapore-private-nft-club-arc-teams-up-with-millennium-hotelsnft-club-arc-teams-up-with-millennium-hotels

RICK PARKHILL
Brand Storytelling – A Perfect Storm

In early 2015, friends who worked in the 'digital video' space started encouraging me to launch an event for brands alongside the Sundance Film Festival in Park City, Utah. My entire career has been in B2B media companies with a focus on digital media, including InfoText, Digitrends and iMedia Communications. I had some experience producing business events that catered to brands, but I didn't quite understand the connection between brands and Sundance, the most iconic celebration of independent filmmaking in North America.

It sounded more like a fun reason to visit Park City, do some skiing, and catch some films. It took me a minute to understand that brands were beginning to see the future where digital natives were not receptive to having their media choices interrupted. The media strategy discussions were beginning to look at alternatives to the 30-second spot.

The most desired consumers were watching content on their own terms and that did not include ads. The stampede to streaming platforms was growing louder. Influencer marketing was becoming a real thing. Brand YouTube channels were becoming a necessity. The writing on the wall was becoming clear; brands need to create content that informs, entertains, and inspires.

They need to attract audiences rather than interrupt them. They need to tell great stories that will compete in a crowded media environment. They need to partner with the best storytellers and creators and guess what? Those folks show up enforce each January in Park City, Utah for the Sundance Film Festival.

The first Brand Storytelling event in 2016 brought 50+ major brands together for three days of panels and presentations designed to help navigate the rapidly evolving media environment and present paths to create quality content. In 2016, many brands were making meager investments in creating content for their owned media, mostly their own websites and YouTube. But there were lots of aspirational conversations that cracked open the door for brand investment in high quality entertainment projects.

RICK PARKHILL
Brand Storytelling – A Perfect Storm

Fast-forward to 2022 and the first-ever Brand Storytelling Theater was founded. Over 150 submissions were considered by a selection committee of brands, agencies, directors, and producers. Fourteen films were selected to screen in Park City and, although the in-person event would be cancelled due to Covid, these films were honoured and screened virtually along with Zoom panels featuring brands and their production partners.

The quality of these films speaks for themselves and the poignant reality that the media world would never be the same. Generations of 'old' traditional media models are rapidly eroding, forcing marketers to become what people seek rather than interrupting what they have found. In just seven years, many brands have emerged as great storytellers, creating content that competes. In fact, this year MailChimp took home an Academy Award for their short film, *The Long Goodbye*. The past few years has seen a tremendous investment by brands in partnering with seasoned creators and filmmakers to create outstanding branded content. Just explore these Official Selections from the Brand Storytelling Theater 2022:

The Show – PepsiCo

The Show is a 90-minute documentary that takes audiences on the creative journey behind The Weeknd's 2021 Pepsi Super Bowl Halftime Show. Proving that it takes a village to pull off an epic cultural moment, the film introduces viewers to the talented professionals - from producers to choreographers - as they join forces to produce the most watched 12-minutes on television – the Superbowl Halftime show.

Black Boys – Procter & Gamble/Old Spice

Black Boys celebrates the full spectrum of humanity of Black men and boys in America while showcasing the social and emotional effects of racism and invites audiences to imagine a world in which Black boys experience true belonging and unlimited possibilities.

The Beauty of Blackness – Sephora

This film chronicles the checkered past, present and future of Black Beauty. It calls attention to the historical and still persistent dearth of fashion and beauty products made for and by people of colour.

RICK PARKHILL
Brand Storytelling – A Perfect Storm

Nian – Apple

Entirely shot on iPhone, the 12-minute movie *Nian* is an alternative take on a Chinese New Year folklore story.

The Park Bench – Aflac

The Park Bench film is a story about family, care and hope. As Bella, a young girl, struggles to cope with her father's Sickle Cell diagnosis, she is befriended by an unlikely ally who lends a helping hand (or wing). The uplifting film was written and directed by Academy Award-nominated, Rob Edwards and produced by Academy Award-winning animation company Lion Forge (creators of *Hair Love*).

Learning To Drown – The North Face

Jess Kimura, considered one of the most influential female snowboarders in the world, was at the top of her career when she lost the love of her life. *Learning to Drown* follows this story of love and loss while showcasing Kimura's determination to fight back for her life.

North Country – Merrell/Burton/The North Face/Icelantic/Keen/Kuhl/Prana/Lahouts

North Country tells the story of America's oldest ski shop, and the journey of the Lahouts family, Lebanese immigrants that have prevailed for a century, with the help of multiple generations of family, who have spent their entire lives working at the shop, they've made it through. Anthony Lahout goes home to spend time with his grandfather Joe, the founder of the Lahout's Ski Shop, for his final years and learns much more than just how to run a shop.

The Way Of The Wildcard – Red Bull

How a girl from a remote Nepali village became a world-class trail runner. This film is about a woman trail runner looking for a way out, who found immense success in something she has always loved to do.

A Woman's Place – KitchenAid

This film brings to life the story of three women: a butcher, a chef and

RICK PARKHILL
Brand Storytelling – A Perfect Storm

a restaurateur, carving out a place for themselves in the male-dominated culinary industry.

Dear Santa – United States Postal Service

The film shines a light on the 100-year-old 'Operation Santa' Program of the United States Postal Service. Each year, hundreds of thousands of letters addressed to Santa Claus arrive at Post Offices around the country. This film captures some of those heart-warming letters and the stories of how children's wishes were made to come true.

Generation Impact: The Coder – HP

Generation Impact is a video series from the Garage by HP, which spotlights young people with exceptional talents. Motivated by the problems they see in the world, these inspiring minds mesh together a love of science with a dedication to helping others.

Ka Huaka'i: The Journey to Merrie Monarch – Hawaiian Airlines

Every spring since 1971, the best hula hālau are invited to Hilo, Hawaii to perform in the most prestigious hula competition of its kind: the Merrie Monarch Festival. The film follows the journey of three hula practitioners - a teacher, a chanter, and a dancer - as they prepare to step onto the stage.

Who Is a Runner: Prolyfyck Run Crew – Brooks Running

Following racist events in their community, a running group sets out to change the image of their neighborhood and people who live there. This is the first in a series of videos by Brooks and Camp4 Collective.

Not The Science Type – 3M

Not The Science Type is a docuseries featuring four female scientists as they rise to prominence in fields including micro-biology and nuclear engineering, challenging stereotypes and confronting gender, race and age discrimination along the way. These films range from a 3-minute animated short to a 90-minute feature and are all worth viewing to gain a clear perspective of the state of brand storytelling today.

RICK PARKHILL
Brand Storytelling – A Perfect Storm

Some trends worth noting:

> - **Documentaries are the flavour of the day**
> - **Purpose-driven storytelling is becoming far more prevalent**
> - **Quality of production is rising**
> - **Top directors from film and TV are being recruited for brand-funded projects**
> - **Multiple 'partners' are being deployed for the development and production, i.e., advertising and PR agencies, production companies, content studios**
> - **Brand aspiration to create on-going series that build on-going audiences versus one-off films**

We are witnessing a 'perfect brand storytelling storm' that has been building for years now and it is likely to become more powerful in the years ahead as brands become more comfortable with the process of creating and distributing this type of content. It's an exciting time as media, marketing and entertainment collides.

Rick Parkhill is the Founder of InfoText, Digitrends, iMedia and BrandStorytelling. Rick is a B2B media entrepreneur and observer, who is infatuated with the impact of media and technology on culture and society. He is a producer of over 100 advertising and media events, publisher, and journalist. Currently, Director of Brand Storytelling, an associate event of the Sundance Film Festival.

SYLVIA ENOTIADES
The Evolution Of Influencer Marketing

I am honoured to have been asked as a contributor marking the twenty-year anniversary of the branded content story and to have been part of the BCMA. When I embarked on my social media journey, I never envisioned that I would be at the forefront of such an explosive industry, Influencer Marketing. In short, I will touch on all the aspects of significance during my 7-year career exposure and the evolution of Influencer Marketing.

It all started in 2016, when I was scouting for Influencers to fulfil a branding campaign, it wasn't an easy task due to the lack of searchability and it being a fully manual process as the likes of technology platforms were in their infancy. Finding the relevant influencers across social platforms and channels was more complicated as they were few and far between, there was a lack of niche and vertical specific creators, but this isn't a problem today. We also had to contend with not knowing whether they were ridden with fake followers or not. Speaking from a seller's point as someone who worked for a well-known Influencer Marketing platform, trying to deliver customer/branded campaigns was often a challenge.

For example, looking for automotive creators was nearly impossible. During the campaign, we were unable to fulfil the requirements necessary to meet the targets and KPI's, luckily, we encouraged the client to pivot their audience category allowing us to approach lifestyle, family and travel influencers broadening the reach. In the earlier days, to engage a creator who was classified as a 'celebrity' for e.g., race car drivers, was not simple as the novelty of branded influencer partnerships were not a consideration. Fast-forward to today and there are now more automotive creator options than we can choose to work with.

On the other hand, could the unlimited creator options be seen as something negative? Personally, I don't think so. The constant growth and evolution of the market keeps the creators in check, and this can be seen as a way of managing the creator economy. It takes a lot of work as a creator to be relevant, by doing so they need to ensure their content is fresh and appealing. Their biggest challenge is to ensure that they don't lose their source of income.

SYLVIA ENOTIADES
The Evolution Of Influencer Marketing

Once they lose their staying power, they also lose out financially.

The different and numerous social platforms have been instrumental in creator success and growth of the industry. The industry giant, Meta, has championed the creative output across Facebook and Instagram. Twitter has always been steady but less used since this has remained a channel of choice more for informative and reactive content.

Twitter has long been favoured more for business-to-business interactions, similarly to LinkedIn, with the rise of Key Opinion Leaders who remain influential within their industries but tend to stick to these more preferred channels. These KOL's are aspirational due to having built their following on these specific channels.

The most recent challenger business to come onto the scene is TikTok, its short-form video content attracted new users, propelling it to be the most adopted and best performing channel since launch. TikTok has managed to attract a new audience which Meta was seemingly losing and unable to retain. This has also caused other industry giants such as YouTube and Instagram to react in their offerings, to retain their current users. YouTube launched 'YouTube Shorts', a better way for their users to consume shorter-form content without losing their fan base to other competitor channels.

Instagram announced 'Reels', in a bid to save their consumer base from moving over to TikTok. Instagram has also faced backlash over the years due to continued algorithmic changes which has significantly impacted creator growth and vanity metrics. TikTok has catered to these needs, thanks to their algorithm promoting content that is not due to the number of followers, but more based on creativity.

Furthermore, there are less constraints when it comes to music rights usage, something that Instagram doesn't seem to favour. Conclusively, each platform has their advantages as they cater to multiple wants and needs, plus the demand is greater than ever. We know that there are at least 50 million creators globally who are making use of these platforms in numerous ways, meaning that there is a constant need for developments and offerings to retain interest.

Presently, it appears TikTok is leading the way in this sense with their creator marketplace, which enables their users to gain control allowing their needs to be fed back into the business and implemented based on the creator's requirements.

SYLVIA ENOTIADES
The Evolution Of Influencer Marketing

As the social channels continue to evolve, so has the need for creative content. Gone are the days when brands or clients could prescribe their specific briefs and demand total creative control. If we think about what content used to look like, an influencer could be standing there with a bottle of Coca-Cola blatantly taking up ⅓ of the image, but as branded leniency and understanding has changed, this now has allowed the creators to become like an extension of their marketing team.

Branded posts have become less noticeable and ultimately, ads have performed better overall for creator and brand. Consequently, this has prompted for more transparency within the industry to ensure disclaimers are clear when content is branded by using #ad. Moreover, it has allowed for brands and agencies to utilise this content for their content asset banks across multiple different streams of advertising.

Certainly, the advancement of technology has shown that even content shot using a smart phone is of as good quality when compared to some of the content created by advertising agencies who would charge a premium. There are several brands who have boldly and bravely hired creators to star in, shoot and direct on their productions to be utilised for TVC's which usually would harbour a much higher cost when done using the more traditional routes.

The rise of the Influencer Marketing industry has seen the increase and emergence of new businesses looking to cash in on the latest advertising trend, meaning there is now more competition as they battle for the same budgets.

My background lies within the platform/influencer technology sector, and we are constantly observing these new market entries. However, few have the staying power and the expertise to invest where needed to adapt to client needs and requirements, as well as maintaining their understanding of the ever-changing social landscape.

Overall, the growth of the borderless society has had a significant and beneficial impact for both creators and brands across the globe. Seemingly, brands have become more discoverable than ever before and in turn the talent pool has increased. We have witnessed brands who were losing their customer base be re-invigorated by collaborating with the creator of the moment. These creator collaborations have seen brands increase their ROI and attract a younger more affluent consumer economy and we don't see this slowing down.

SYLVIA ENOTIADES
The Evolution Of Influencer Marketing

This incremental growth benefits all the social channels, the influencer platforms and marketing businesses, as well as allowing it to close the loop on international expansion and connections. I can't wait to see where the next 20 years are going to take us, and I am excited to be a part of this emerging industry as it becomes seen as a new revenue stream in the more traditional advertising areas.

Sylvia Enotiades is Head of UK, Country Manager at Izea, a marketing technology company providing software and professional services that enable brands to collaborate and transact with the full spectrum of top social influencers and content creators. Sylvia is driven and hard working and always willing to accept a challenge. A superb multi-tasker, organised with a team-oriented attitude. She is a passionate foodie that is aspiring to better my food knowledge and work in this ever-growing industry. She loves all things social media and food and is the co-Founder of a budding food Instagram account @twofoodiesnodiet

JESSICA MILLOWICK
Making A Market That Works For Talent And Brands

Athletes are increasingly in demand for brand endorsements, which means marketers need a complete view of the talent market to seize the right opportunities.

Sport is a celebration of talent

Fans love to watch the best at their best. In the digital age, the biggest stars animate global communities and bring all kinds of people together.

Naturally, brands and media companies want to be a part of that – they want a part of the audiences that talent can generate. The marketplace is getting bigger; opportunities have grown more abundant.

That is a brilliant thing. But it is not without its challenges. Everyone wants choices but nobody wants to be overloaded with obligations – least of all athletes striving for optimum performance.

Safraz Ali is the head of marketing and communications at Roc Nation Sports International, an entertainment company that grows athletes' profiles out of their personalities and cultural interests. For him, the biggest challenge is prioritisation.

> *"There are so many things that get thrown at athletes. Media opportunities, commercial deals, on-pitch matters – and, of course, they're humans, so everything that comes with that."*
> **Safraz Ali, Head Of Marketing & Communications, Roc Nation Sports International**

Efficiency and harmony are crucial in talent management. Dysfunctional processes do not help anyone. Deliverables go missing, individuals burn out and relationships suffer.

So it has never been more important to develop an ecosystem that puts the value of talent at the centre.

JESSICA MILLOWICK
Making A Market That Works For Talent And Brands

Pickstar's online talent marketplace lets brands and companies find the right individual for any public appearance, speaking opportunity or campaign.

The VLAST platform, meanwhile, centralises communications and data about every active campaign, so that teams, agents and brand partners are all on the same page.

Talent at the heart of sport

There are few better examples of talent's growing influence than in rugby union, a trend reflected in Roc Nation's own activities.

It has been working with the United Rugby Championship, which features leading clubs from Ireland, Scotland, Wales, Italy, and South Africa.

Together, they have been building a greater sense of identity, and centring storytelling on the performers at the heart of the competition.

Roc Nation has also signed up exciting stars like England's Ellis Genge, combining engaging personalities with rugby's traditions of commitment and responsibility. It is a sport where talent is being taken more seriously.

These are interesting times for rugby union. On the one hand, the post-Covid period has brought profound economic challenges to the professional structure. In England, the financial plight of Wasps and Worcester Warriors has shown just how difficult things can get.

There are some complex, far-reaching conversations taking place about funding and the role of different stakeholders in the future. What seems certain, however, is that the players will be at the forefront of the era to come.

No one can afford to miss out on the value of talent and the partnerships built around it. Streamlining activations, branded content and personal appearances can prevent teams getting overstretched.

That can free creative people to flourish, and maybe even unlock added extras that inspire new collaborations.

JESSICA MILLOWICK
Making A Market That Works For Talent And Brands

Finding time for talent

That uncertainty aside, rugby union is hitting an epic run of events. The women's edition of the Rugby World Cup is happening now in New Zealand, setting new attendance and audience records.

In the northern hemisphere, the calendar is also heating up. This year's autumn internationals will showcase the heavyweights of men's union ahead of their own Rugby World Cup in France in 2023.

It's a setting from which new heroes will emerge and there will be some incredible stories to be told.

And that is true far beyond rugby. We are barely a month away from an unprecedented FIFA World Cup in Qatar, happening midway through the European football season – a tournament that will magnetise global attention while complicating the schedules of the stars involved. Next year, Australia and New Zealand will host the FIFA Women's World Cup, giving even more female footballers a platform at a time of amazing momentum in their sport.

In cricket, the men's T20 World Cup is about to get underway in Australia, ahead of the most crowded season so far for franchise leagues. Twelve months from now, that sport's biggest event, the men's 50-over Cricket World Cup, will head to its biggest market, India.

Everywhere we look, we see the same challenge: capitalising on a point of maximum opportunity in a historically busy period.

> *"They are athletes first and foremost, and it's because of the success they enjoy on the pitch that we're able to do the off-field activities. What they do off-field should complement their incredible achievements on the field, so the two definitely work hand-in-hand. When the fixtures get congested, it's difficult to get certain opps or deliverables over the line so, it's about planning ahead and being proactive when it comes to scheduling these types of appearances, shoots and opps."*
>
> Safraz Ali, Head Of Marketing & Communications, Roc Nation Sports International

JESSICA MILLOWICK
Making A Market That Works For Talent And Brands

For athletes hitting a new peak, it is also about the right deal – not just the deal right now. There is a balance to be struck between making the most of a moment in time and building authentic, meaningful partnerships that connect personally and commercially.

Opportunity only means so much if you have no way of seizing it. With the right tools, and the right approach, it is possible to make talent count.

Jessica Millowick is Chief Operating Officer at PickStar, the world's fastest growing self-serve marketplace platform linking brands, fans, agencies, and businesses with talent. She is also CCO at sister brand, VLAST, the leading AI, machined learned talent management platform utilised by some of sport's biggest rights owners, including the NFL, MLSE, and AFL. Jess runs and manages all operations, people, and functional teams across the two businesses, globally, with reports in Australia, Europe, and North America. She has a robust knowledge of global technology, sports, and entertainment markets, influencer marketing, and UX. Jess is a respected business leader with an entrepreneurial flair and problem solving mindset which has helped her support the rapid growth of both brands over the last six years.

DR RULA AL ABDULRAZAK
Is Branded Content Capable Of Increasing A Brand's Inclusivity?

We live a 'Branded life'. As we dress, eat, and select our relationships, our perception of how we are perceived is on our minds, consciously or subconsciously. When we exist, speak and behave, others assess us based on their experiences that associate behaviours, words, and body language with specific meanings. We do the same as we envision how they are judging us. What we imagine is not necessarily what they perceive, but both influence our behaviours. The-Self-Concept (Rogers, 1951) represents this fact through the actual-self, ideal-self, and social-self. Reality is subjective with brands; what we perceive to be true is true. Big brands realise the potential in the way they engage with society. They managed to access audiences' homes, minds, and hearts through media.

In its traditional and creative outlets, media is a vital source of affirmation for our sense of worth. While media inform and entertain, tailored information tends to be shared with targeted audiences. Targeting audiences and creatively encoding relevant and meaningful stories and achieving the marketers' goal can exclude and marginalise others. Targeting is discriminatory in nature and is key in brand-sponsored-contents.

Branded content is either funded or produced by marketers (Hardy, 2021). Engaging in the production of entertainment and artistic mediums embeds brands deeper in the fabric of people's lives, enhances brand awareness and establishes brand associations.

Red Bull is considered a branded content leader, utilising various media vehicles, including TV and online films, journalistic publications, and sponsoring and creating sports events partnering with a wide range of brands. Red Bull's brand value is enforced by engaging in high-adrenaline and adventurous sports. The brand partners with niche brands, such as L39ION of LA cycling team.

The film 'A Mission to change cycling' (Red Bull, 2022) offers meaningful insight into the journey of the black athletic team and Justine Williams.

DR RULA AL ABDULRAZAK
Is Branded Content Capable Of Increasing A Brand's Inclusivity?

It enables Red Bull to show a more inclusive culture after being challenged in the media by the leak of a racist marketing map image presented by their global culture director in 2020 and their silent response to Black Lives Matter and George Floyd's murder (Moses, 2020).

Although the brand benefited from associations with Black culture, it was reported that the company culture did not seem to reflect that, and the black community was not supported by the company (Johnson and Rodriguez, 2020). 'Whitewashing' is one of the hidden prejudice practices where brands thrive through the inspiration of a specific culture, such as black culture and hip hop, then select white characters to represent it.

Branded content can have a profound impact on society. Educating audiences by addressing important social causes such as microaggression. In 2020 Vox. Creative's Explainer Studio engaged in an inclusivity project with Qatar Foundation offering a meaningful resource that shows what branded content can achieve. This partnership created an in-depth video featuring remote interviews with students and educators worldwide, sharing vulnerable and personal stories about why mispronouncing a name can undermine a student's identity and impact their education (Vox Creative, 2020).

Amazon's 'One night in Miami' film imagines meaningful conversations between historical black icons addressing their struggles in the late 1950s, which associates Amazon with diverse and inclusive cultural values that support equity. Netflix's paid post in the New York Times promoting the 'Orange is the new Black' series discusses why the male model to run prisons does not work for women inmates, which also addresses an important equity issue in society.

Branded content in these examples is very helpful in developing social understanding and encouraging inclusive practices. Such content also forms a positive association with the brands among the supported communities. Whether the brands practice and live these values or not is more complex. Amazon, for example, has been accused of systemic racism (Larson, 2021).

To what extent are the audiences consuming the film aware of the accusation? Are brands developing an inclusive organisational culture as they raise social awareness, or is it propaganda? It's ethically problematic if brands do not live the values they are preaching yet benefit from the associations.

DR RULA AL ABDULRAZAK
Is Branded Content Capable Of Increasing A Brand's Inclusivity?

Inclusive brands are not limited to more inclusive advertising because segmenting and targeting are discriminatory in nature. Inclusive brands are a result of inclusive organisational identity and culture. I aspire in my work with brands to enable them to create an inclusive organisation and teams who can produce inclusive brands.

Moreover, the boundaries between brands and media content are blurry, and media consumers may not consciously realise the role of the sponsor in encoding the message they are consuming or of the brand associations it is creating in their minds.

Regulations that clearly highlight brands and sponsors' roles and any conflict of interest in media and journalism content are important. Is there a sufficient balance of share of voice? Better brand practices for applying the regulations are also needed. The media and brands need to hold themselves accountable to live by the values they are communicating and to enable a wider and balanced share of voice.

References

Hardy, J. (2021). Branded Content: the fateful merging of media and marketing. London: Routledge

Johnson, L. and Rodriguez, A. (2020). Insiders at Complex Networks said the company was built on Black culture but that the sales team 'whitewashed' advertising deals for brands, replacing black people with white people in pitch decks. Business Insider. Available at:

https://www.businessinsider.com/complex-networks-insiders-says-sales-team-whitewashed-ad-deals-2020-7?r=US&IR=T. (Accessed on 28 October 2022).

Larson, E. (2021). Amazon sued for alleged race, gender bias in corporate hires. Bloomberg UK. Available at:

https://www.bloomberg.com/news/articles/2021-03-01/amazon-is-sued-for-alleged-racial-and-gender-discrimination?leadSource=uverify%20wall. (Accessed on 29 October 2022).

Moses, L. (2020). Some companies that thrived because of Black culture are being called out for hypocrisy. Business Insider.com. Available at: https://www.businessinsider.com/complex-networks-red-bull-face-scrutiny-over-diversity-newsletter-2020-7?r=US&IR=T. (Accessed on 28 October 2022).

Red Bull. (2022). A Mission to Change Cycling: Justin Williams & L39ION of LA. Red Bull Bike. YouTube Channel. Available at: https://www.youtube.com/watch?v=EK7WkUfrr28. (Accessed on 28 October 2022).

Rogers, C. (1951). Client-centered therapy: Its current practice, implications, and theory. London: Constable.

Vox Creative. (2020). Why mispronouncing a name can undermine a student's identity and how to help. Vox. Available at: https://www.vox.com/ad/21272071/name-mispronunciation-student-education-microaggression-classroom. (Accessed 28 October 2022).

Dr Rula Al Abdulrazak is a Senior Lecturer in International Marketing and Branding at the Royal Docks School of Business and Law, University of East London. Prior to academia, Rula held consultancy and specialist positions at a European Commission Business Centre and at AFPC/Shell operating company on the Mediterranean. Rula is interested in creativity and reflexivity in teaching, learning, self-development, coaching, brand design, marketing, and business growth. She enjoys utilising art and oil painting, creative writing poem and short stories in the process and celebrating better understanding and awareness of emotions and human psychology. She practises positive psychology and coaching with individuals and teams. She has also undertaken consultancy in branding, global marketing, positive leadership, and systemic coaching.

REBECCA ALLEN
Harnessing The Voice Of Your Customer

I am about to reveal an uncomfortable truth. Over the very many years I've worked in content marketing, I have frequently heralded the increasing maturity of the discipline.

As innovation and creativity has exploded in the space, smart technology has superpowered our ability to reach and engage audiences at a staggering scale. The number of industry award categories dedicated to success in the field is testament to the fact that it has earned its rightful place in the upper echelons of marketing prowess. And for good reason; focusing on providing value through education, entertainment or inspiration is both worthy and worth it (thanks L'Oreal). So, we can now rest assured that, unlike many forms of advertising, content earns us real engagement and loyalty from our previously ambivalent target audiences.

Right?

Sorry, wrong. Because here's the truth; *they still don't really trust you. You're a brand, and they know it.*

With consumer cynicism at an undeniable all-time high, building and retaining trust is harder than it has ever been. Brand love is at best fickle, at worst a mythical creature.

Now, this is not to say you are wasting your time and budget on content marketing, far from it. But even the most creative and innovative branded content strategies in the world could be missing a fundamental component that could bring you closer to your audience, building trust whilst dramatically increasing ROI.

Harnessing the voice of your advocate customer.

I'm not necessarily referring to traditional 'influencers' here, but rather the people that spontaneously and voluntarily enthuse about your brand or products across social media.

REBECCA ALLEN
Harnessing The Voice Of Your Customer

Here's the thing; ever since people have bought anything, word-of-mouth has been both a blessing and a curse for the companies selling to them. Businesses have frequently lived or died on the strength of both scathing reviews and glowing recommendations.

Conversations about your products and services are happening all the time, completely out of your control. Today, they are happening at a staggering speed and scale across an ever-changing social media landscape. As overwhelming as this can seem, it also represents a huge content opportunity, especially for direct-to-consumer brands.

Discovering and amplifying user-generated content (UGC) from your unprompted fans can be a very powerful tool in making many elements of your digital content programme work harder. Integrating republished posts and video content on your owned and paid media channels can greatly deepen engagement. Utilising relevant content on product pages and in abandoned shopping cart emails has been proven to dramatically increase sales conversion. And by interacting with your advocates, it is also possible to build authentic communities around your brand which opens up to many more opportunities, from research and development to co-creation.

Given the sheer scale and unpredictable nature of UGC, it is near impossible for brands of any size to manage this in-house. But over recent years, smart technology has emerged to help. Platforms such as Miappi, Stackla and Bazaar Voice allow marketers to source, curate and publish content to their owned and paid channels, as well as manage permission from their advocates. Case studies from Miappi for example, who work with the likes of Unilever and Millennium Hotels globally, cite engagement uplift of 24% when organic customer content is utilised in paid advertising campaigns.

In the eCommerce space there is mounting evidence from a variety of sources, that the presence of UGC on product pages increases sales conversion by between 43% to a whopping 106%. Not surprising when you consider the IAB's finding that it is trusted on average 50% more than regular advertising.

As part of your overall branded content mix, it is well worth considering how integrating the voice of your customer could make your own content creation efforts work that much harder. It provides a transparency and authenticity that can only help you build trust, and ultimately deliver ROI.

REBECCA ALLEN
Harnessing The Voice Of Your Customer

And there is of course a marvellous side benefit to this way of listening to your customers and understanding what they care about. Because by harnessing the positive sentiment of a proactive community you can create content that you have more certainty of hitting the mark. And maybe, get more of them caring about you.

Rebecca Allen is a dynamic business leader with 20-years of experience in the digital marketing sector, 12 years of which have been in the branded content space both in the UK and globally. Having held senior positions spearheading business development and commercial growth at BrightTALK, Outbrain, The Drum, and Codec. She has vast experience working with both B2B and B2C businesses and brands, as well as their agencies. In addition to content marketing, she also has a real passion for disruptive technologies that have the potential to supercharge it. She holds several Non-Executive Director positions and is Chair of the Board of Positive News. Rebecca is a BCMA Global Advisor and Board Director.

JULIE DARDOUR
Content Lover: A Life Of Passion

I spent more than 15 years in the press, I then created my own content marketing agency and I spent 5 years with different advertisers (Coty and Mars) as Global Chief Content Officer. Today I am the head of The House of Content, a consulting and recruitment firm dedicated to the content industry.

Through the different roles I've held, I've seen content evolve greatly, but especially in recent years when we could talk about a Content Revolution. This last one I explain by two phenomena: social media and retail media/retail content which have completely changed the way content is organised in companies.

When I was working in the general press industry, the editor-in-chief told me that there were always two ways to celebrate an anniversary. Either look back or look forward. For the occasion of BCMA's 20th anniversary, I wanted to share with you my vision of how Content will be written in the years to come.

We will only talk about Content and no longer about branded content, brand content...all the typologies (brand content, product content, corporate content, etc...) and all the definitions of content will be grouped under one single term: CONTENT

Content will be elevated to a strategic function and no longer to the role of content production. Content marketers will be the new marketing officers. The content professions are multiplying and will become increasingly senior, led by Chief Content Officers (strategy, production, dissemination, and measurement) and the organisational charts will be modified.

Agencies specialising in content and senior experts will multiply, with expertise and skills that are more 'media' and editorial management, to the disadvantage of communication agencies, who will be seen as being too generalist.

We will finally have found the formula to calculate what content investments really represent in companies

JULIE DARDOUR
Content Lover: A Life Of Passion

(one of the major projects of BCMA France) and thus we will be able to calculate the ROI easily which will help the financiers and the executive committees of each company to fund more content projects.

The so-called content tech solutions will have a more important place in the whole value chain and the most laborious tasks will continue to be replaced by artificial intelligence (AI). There will be a growing gap between AI-based content products and Hero Content, which will allow companies to focus on higher quality content.

Less is more: norms and standards will emerge to produce less and better content. The responsibility to produce content sensibly (especially in terms of carbon footprint) will be one of the indicators of success for content marketers

Content marketers will become more and more numerous and we will need organisations like the BCMA to really orchestrate this Content Revolution!

Happy birthday BCMA and so proud to be part of you!!!

Julie Dardour is the Founder of The House Of Content, a consulting and recruitment firm dedicated to the content industry. Prior to this she was Global Content Strategy & Operations Director at Royal Canin, a division of Mars. After 15 years in media as Sales and Marketing Directors (Condé Nast group, Vogue, GQ, Glamour, Libération, Radio Nova), Julie created her own content agency LiGNE 26, dedicated to luxury and lifestyle content. She joined Coty Group in 2017 as Global Content and Digital director for Lancaster beauty and Escada. Julie created the first Brand Content MBA in France in 2011 at Sup. De pub, where she regularly gives content marketing classes. Julie is Vice President and Secretary of BCMA France and this year she is leading the launch of the first Content Observatory in France.

ADAM HARRIS
How Do You Do, Fellow Marketers

Throughout history, the youngest demographic with purchasing power are the ones that create the largest behavioural shifts in society. Over the last 20-years, millennials have ruled the demographic roost. Diving headfirst, often without fear for their own safety, into the vast, connected, data harvesting worlds of social media. Where this powerful cohort went, branded content followed with seemingly endless opportunities and new and ever-changing rules of engagement.

As the BCMA enters the impressive landmark of its 20th year, we appear to be at the start of the next big generational transformation. I witnessed this demographic shift first-hand 20-years ago while heading up the branded content team at the millennial innovation that was Metro Newspapers. And I'm seeing it again now at Twitch as millennials pass the demographic baton over to Gen Z. We are seeing key shifts in cultural codes and values of this next power generation. Moving away from individualised social amplification that social media provides, to far more community, connected, decentralised experiences, often born in gaming environments, but now broadening across content and culture.

This is the reason for the growth of the likes of Twitch, Reddit, Discord and Tik Tok and the reason we are seeing significant shifts in approach by legacy social media companies, such as Facebook, with their multi-billion-dollar rebranding to Meta. A clear play to garner a new, younger audience that already exists in this online universe of content, gaming, and connection. I view this as an implied acknowledgment that to win at scale you need the youngest, most powerful demographic.

Forming a large part of this emerging audience are Gen Z: the latest trendsetters coming of age. Born between 1997 and 2012 they are currently between 10 and 25-years old. They are the latest generation to enter the spotlight and are ready to start exerting influence, emerging with even greater impact thanks to the pandemic. According to Business Insider, Gen Z are and will be behind social change and conversation for the next 15-years. In a little over a decade, they will have taken over the economy: the 2.5-billion-person generation currently earns $7 trillion, but by 2025 this will be $17 trillion and by 2030, it will be $33 trillion, representing 27% of the world's income.

ADAM HARRIS
How Do You Do, Fellow Marketers

Therefore, it is vitally important for advertisers to build a brand relationship with this audience now to have the right and opportunity to build lifetime value. To achieve this, branded content will continue to be a key weapon in the marketers' armoury. But the rules will be different because this new generation communicates like no other before.

The advancement of technology has an outsized impact on the changing face of communication. Gen Z and even more so their already emerging disciples, Gen Alpha, are an audience who have only ever known a digital world and have always been connected. Digital environments such as Roblox and Fortnite are their playground. They expect their social experiences to be dynamic, in real time and collective. It's no coincidence that these virtual worlds are booming and there is so much talk of the 'metaverse'. Thanks to the advancement of technology and given an almighty nudge by the pandemic, not only are the digital environments where social interaction takes place changing but so are the very means of communication. Take written words as an example. They were shortened by acronyms. They were substituted for emotes. And now memes are a visual language of choice.

With this new generation communicating in a more tacit fashion than ever before, in real time environments that focus more on the community than the individual, branded content and its practitioners will need to adapt and evolve. Not only in the way we tell our stories but also in how we measure their success. Defining value where meaning is implied, in a live moment in time, is tricky to say the least.

I believe you can begin to understand the new rules of the game by analysing the changing cultural codes of the most powerful demographic. This can provide a lens to begin to not only understand how to communicate, but ultimately direct how and what we should value. To celebrate the start of the BCMA's next 20 years, I'd like to harness learning from our work at Twitch to provide some thoughts on how I believe we should now be thinking about branded content in the new demographic landscape.

The first cultural shift we are seeing from this audience is the preference for authentic over curated experiences. This young generation has been brought up in a time of information overload. Authenticity is constantly being questioned whether it's fake news, deep fakes, or algorithmic echo chambers. And most prevalent is the growing realisation that those who are deemed influencers, however relatable they may seem, utilise technology to cultivate a 'projected life'.

ADAM HARRIS
How Do You Do, Fellow Marketers

They do so by selectively curating and sharing only the moments in their lives that are tailored to their specific online identities. Thus, creating a false and in-authentic representation of life and therefore an unattainable picture of happiness. Today's emerging audiences are gradually moving away from this, instead seeking out far more raw, real, and authentic experiences.

For this generation, true happiness lies in being authentically, unapologetically human: celebrating and laughing at our flaws, being true to ourselves and proud to share who we really are – anytime, anywhere. In terms of branded content, this generation reflects their true selves in the content they share online, and they want brands to follow suit. To trust brands, they must first understand what they authentically stand for before they commit and become a loyal customer. Build brand trust through your branded content by demonstrating your authentic human side, welcome spontaneity and embrace the unpolished candour of the live dynamic environments this generation inhabit.

Moving onto the second cultural shift - and our lives and storytelling are moving from fixed to fluid. Until recently the vast amount of our entertainment consumption can be categorised as fixed one-way experiences with minimal opportunity for spontaneity. Movies were linear, video games had clearly defined winners or losers, interaction with traditional sports was limited to going to the event or shouting at the screen either on your own at home or maybe with others in a bar. Thanks to technology, distinctions between the virtual world and IRL are becoming less pronounced and what used to only be physical spontaneity is now transformed digitally.

Movies such as *Bandersnatch* allowed the audience the spontaneity to control the narrative, games like *Among Us* allow for the fluid creation of different stories and characters every time you play. Sports fans can instantly call up any statistic or take advantage of the rise of virtual co-viewing, which can now be found on several streaming services. From a branded content standpoint, this generation has grown up in a technologically advanced society where seemingly nothing is technologically impossible.

They expect that everything should be seamless, fluid and tailored for them. Brands should be thinking about how to take advantage of the creative digital opportunities and most importantly have the storytelling flexibility to create fluid and adaptive narratives.

ADAM HARRIS
How Do You Do, Fellow Marketers

The third cultural shift to guide you is the move from individualistic passive experiences to community and active collaboration. The pandemic highlighted to all generations that with technology we can work, play and interact together like never before.

Today's young audiences know and expect that entertainment can be more than just passively watching content from afar. They want a collective community experience that generates a real sense of unity where everyone laughs together, sometimes cries together, able to meaningfully contribute and support each other. This emerging audience connects and builds their communities around shared values, interests, and passions.

Brands that take a community-first approach will set themselves up for success. To really build loyalty through the togetherness and unity of a community setting, brands need to not only align their values with the community and the community's leaders but add value to that community. They should go beyond passive push interactions and actively encourage participation from a willing community. If you push, they'll invariably push back.

Last but by no means least, my final key behavioural change is also an important change in values. Gen Z see themselves and their values as purposeful and inclusive and expect the same from the brands they engage with. The democratisation of technology, media and education has brought many complex societal issues to the fore and a belief that everyone should be able to take part when it comes to art, culture, learning and entertainment.

Whereas millennials favoured exclusivity and pushed the notion of FOMO (Fear Of Missing Out), this audience value inclusivity and are pushing brands to reflect the diverse voices found within the online barrierless community environments this generation lives in. Today's audiences expect brands to authentically stand for something, not just virtue signal. They want the values of the brands they use and the 'influencers' they follow to match their own. They understand the power of live, interactive environments can have in amplifying a communities' attempts at driving positive change.

People are stronger when they come together, at the same time and same place with shared values and shared missions. In relation to branded content, brands will build love when they invite engagement through collaborations with communities and the influential voices who lead them.

ADAM HARRIS
How Do You Do, Fellow Marketers

A genuine, non-manufactured sense of shared purpose will be the power behind successful Gen Z branded content.

In conclusion, both the audience and the means to reach them are changing at an accelerated pace. The changes we see over the next 20-years I've no doubt will be more revolutionary than at any point in history. And yes, this will require the branded content practitioner to evolve and adapt. But hopefully the above indicates that one thing remains true. Effective branded content does not require you to be a platform expert, a multimedia storyteller, or a member of the youngest most powerful generation (although, as a member of Gen X I admit it is handy to have these in your team).

I argue that great branded content in any era will always originate from the brand storyteller's ability to understand the behaviours of their audience.

The most important branded content skill in the next 20-years will continue to be, being a human. Good luck, fellow marketers.

Adam Harris is the Global Head of the Twitch Brand Partnership Studio. Adam is an award-winning creative leader with 20-years global media experience in the worlds of gaming, sports and entertainment. He advocates for gaming as a significantly untapped marketing opportunity and provides thought leadership on the gamerverse, Generation Z, live streaming and the creator economy. Adam had the honour of Judging the Entertainment category at 2022 Cannes Lions, was named one of the world's top 100 digital marketers in the Drum Digerati 2019 list, appeared in the 2019 #Influencer50 list of the brightest minds in global influencer marketing and has collected a 'Leader In Sport' under 40 award. He is an advisory board member of the Branded Content Marketing Association (BCMA) and is a regular speaker at industry conferences.

KATHERINE ELIZABETH EKRAMI
Is It On Purpose? The Search For Accountability In Purpose Marketing

Purpose-led content and marketing need to be meaningful and meet the growing expectations of consumers and society. The effects of these communications need to be evaluated and refined as a brand's journey evolves. Something we as an industry can do better. Within this short essay, I have identified three key strategies that can create brand accountability, encourage transparency, and improve campaign outcomes for stakeholders.

In recent years, we have seen a surge in brand activism and purpose marketing as brands recognise the importance of using their platform and resources to advocate for social and political issues. Edelman's annual Trust Barometer is just one of the many ways consumers are discontent with the current socio-political climate is being measured. Every year, the expectation for action grows.

From Nike's "Just Do It" campaign featuring Colin Kaepernick to Patagonia's "Vote the Assholes Out", brands are attempting to lead the conversations on some of the world's most critical issues. The ultimate question is, how can we ensure campaigns are beneficial to the causes they champion?

For too long, marketing teams have evaded criticism of woke-washing, co-opting and marketing issues of inequality and social justice without any substance or follow-through earning them undeserved praise and loyalty[1]. Purpose and purpose marketing is now a ubiquitous term within the industry, used to describe how everyday life's seemingly mundane products can positively impact society. Yet, because of a lack of accountability, measurement and impact monitoring, purpose marketing is in danger of becoming another term in the ever-growing backlog of marketing jargon, much like femvertising, corporate social responsibility and cause-related marketing.

With increased public and journalistic scrutiny alongside tools like blockchain technology driving demands for transparency, purpose-driven marketing must be done with integrity.

---

1 Sobande, F. (2019) "Woke-washing: 'intersectional' FEMVERTISING and branding 'woke' bravery," *European Journal of Marketing*, 54(11), pp. 2723–2745

KATHERINE ELIZABETH EKRAMI
Is It On Purpose?
The Search For Accountability In Purpose Marketing

Opportunistic and insincere campaigns are quickly highlighted, and brands are deservedly humbled by vast communities assembled across many social media channels. Medieval public wooden stocks are replaced with a digital barrage of condemnation that will live forever. People may forget, but the internet will not.

We know consumers are more likely to trust and support brands that they perceive as being socially responsible and values-driven. And, campaigns are more likely to be successful when they authentically align with the values and concerns of their target audience[2]. Unfortunately, brands often turn to vanity metrics to evidence impact.

Whilst they have their merit, reach and impressions are brand and customer-centric numbers that only provide information on content's performance rather than the impact on society. This type of stat-washing can undermine a campaign's authenticity and makes it difficult to assess whether content resonated with the audience and persuaded consumers to act or change. To start placing accountability at the forefront of campaigns, I propose three strategies that encourage transparency and can improve campaign outcomes for stakeholders.

1. Co-Creation

There is an obvious need for cultural sensitivity when addressing issues such as race and gender. Pepsi sought to end systemic racism and police brutality with a member of a notorious Blackfishing family and a can of brown sugary, sparkling water in one of the most discussed marketing fails in recent years. Not only is Jenner cast as a White Saviour, but the advert also trivialises all experiences of police brutality and creates a mockery of anti-racism. The brand's co-optation of the protest movement backfired on a colossal scale[3] and Pepsi ultimately pulled the campaign. Content as insensitive as this is not made by, or even consulted with, the people they are targeting. Brands should look to take a stand on social-political issues without selling their product as the solution. Or, in the case of Pepsi, suggest a can of pop presented by a white person can solve police brutality. Collaborating with people who have lived and shared experiences seems obvious, as does researching the sensitivity and triggers around a subject. Yet brands often skip or gloss over these steps.

---

2 Edelman. (2022) "The Trust Barometer: The Cycle of Distrust."
3 The advert was widely criticised by global media outlets, including the New York Times, The Guardian, Washington Post, and trade media, including Insider Business, Marketing Week, AdAge, Campaign and Fast Company.

KATHERINE ELIZABETH EKRAMI
Is It On Purpose?
The Search For Accountability In Purpose Marketing

Culture is powerful and dedicating more places at the table to recognise that can lead to enormous gains for companies and ensure that their purpose-driven strategies drive new thinking and create accountability for the brand.

2. Working with micro-influencers

People are less likely to engage with brand narratives that do not resonate with them on a personal level. Working with content creators can be a valuable strategy, as they craft authentic and compelling connections with the intended audience. Body Shop, Adidas and Patagonia are just a few successful brands that have tapped into the creator economy to highlight social-political issues.

The creator economy has also played a significant role in the evolution of branded content. By providing brands with a diverse and authentic range of voices to collaborate with, content reaches an engaged audience. Micro-influencers with specialised audiences have higher perceived levels of authenticity making content more likely to be shared[4]. Shifting the focus from vanity metrics and focusing on an active, motivated audience is critical for activist and purposeful marketing. A share is good; action is better.

For its 2021 Black History Month campaign, Urban Decay took to TikTok for #BlackBoost, a campaign centring around ten Black paid content creators to create content answering the question "Show me you are making Black history, without telling me you're making Black history." Utilising the stitch feature on the social media platform, the influencers created a diverse narrative of differing lived experiences from different professions, not all of which were from the make-up industry. Utilising emerging content creators in this way not only gave credence to Black influencers, who are notoriously underpaid in comparison to their white counterparts[5], but the campaign was perceived to be genuinely supporting Black culture and creativity.

The brand is known for its inclusivity having added an additional 50 different shades to its make-up range back in 2019. Using trusted voices from within a community, Urban Decay amplified sometimes overlooked voices and, despite admitting that organic traction was more difficult than paid, messages resonated with consumers far more.

---

4 Ehlers, K. (2021) "Micro-influencers: When smaller is better." Forbes Magazine.
5 SevenSix Agency. (2021) "Lifting the Lid: The Influencer Pricing Report."

KATHERINE ELIZABETH EKRAMI
Is It On Purpose?
The Search For Accountability In Purpose Marketing

On the back of the campaign, other content creators on TikTok created similar videos; however, they did not adopt the hashtag, indicating that metrics are not always a reliable form of performance. As culture evolves, the journey towards becoming a more purposeful brand is ongoing.

Listening to communities and involving members to amplify their voices through content whilst embedding retrospective and evaluative processes is the only way to see true impact.

3. Being in conversation with your audience

Consumer identity is dynamic. The things communities care about change, and to stay relevant, so must brands. As Henry Jenkins[6] posits, there needs to be a Chief Cultural Officer in every board room to be engrossed in the culture that surrounds your brand.

Identifying that supermarkets play a social role for consumers experiencing loneliness, Dutch supermarket Jumbo launched the 'Slow Checkout Lanes', providing an option for customers to engage in a chat and adopt a more leisurely pace to pay for their goods.

First introduced in 2019, the overwhelmingly positive reception of the initiative has meant that over 200 slow checkouts will be rolled out across the Netherlands, a figure expected to increase in a post-pandemic society.

Creating safe spaces for customers emphasises the need for human contact and that digital solutionism is not always what people want. The supermarket chain's understanding of its customers' emotions clearly aligns with its purpose of being a family-run business at the heart of the community. Only a brand that understands its role in the community can listen and act in such a way.

The concept of purpose-driven marketing will likely evolve and grow. Brands must stay attuned to emerging trends and find creative ways to leverage them in their marketing efforts. This should include embracing the shift towards "conscious capitalism", which aligns commercial success with purposeful motives.

---

6 Kozinets, R.V. and Jenkins, H. (2021) "Consumer movements, Brand Activism, and the participatory politics of Media: A Conversation," Journal of Consumer Culture, 22(1), pp. 264–282.

KATHERINE ELIZABETH EKRAMI
Is It On Purpose?
The Search For Accountability In Purpose Marketing

By doing so, brands can not only improve their reputation and build trust with their audience but also positively impact the world.

Katherine is a freelance strategist and UX writer. She started her career at global agencies, including McCann, specialising in PR. Within a few years, Katherine moved into content strategy and UX, crafting simple user interactions for complex B2B offerings. Katherine is currently undertaking a PhD in brand activism at the University of Arts London. Awarded a Collaborative Doctoral Award by techne, part of the Arts and Humanities Research Council (AHRC), the project's partners include the Branded Content Marketing Association (BCMA), Unilever and GOOD Agency. Katherine is also a qualified teacher and can recall an excessive amount of Buffy the Vampire Slayer trivia.

EMILY BULL
The Time Is Right For Branded Video Content

Over the last decade, I have found the branded video content conversation with my clients has changed. A decade ago, I was explaining why every brand needed a branded content video strategy and needed to start making video content. Today, every brand understands that video must be at the core of their communications strategy. Our conversations now focus on effectiveness, authenticity, and content length. As the market has become comfortable with video as an essential part of their content strategy, the quality, tonality, and effectiveness of video has become the real focus.

Brands are increasingly relying on data to evaluate their content, but they tend to only look at each video individually instead of examining video usage through a comprehensive video strategy to understand the overall impact on brand uplift and connection. This approach misses the chance to factor in emotional connection, storytelling, brand alignment, and authenticity.

The trend towards bite-sized content is driven by better statistical performance on a video-by-video basis, as brands measure views and engagement in isolation. But this rationale for bite-sized content often misses the bigger picture.

Now, this will be an unpopular opinion, but, in my view, bite-sized content, might be easy to consume and share, but it often lacks the depth and substance needed to truly engage and connect with audiences. If content lacks a story or a purposeful message, it can appear shallow and insincere, lacking the ability to make a lasting impact and damaging the development of the brand's narrative and voice.

Video that takes time to tell a story and connect with audiences on an emotional level is more effective in driving deeper engagement and conversions that create brand loyalty and connection.

EMILY BULL
The Time Is Right For Branded Video Content

While we humans like to think we're in control, making decisions based on logic and rational thought, we're not. Up to 90%[1] of our [financial] decisions are based on emotion.

NRMA Insurance, an Australian insurance brand, recognises the power of emotional video content and consistent strategies. Its goal is to inspire all Australians to be proactive in preparing for extreme weather events and to build stronger communities. To achieve this, the brand has launched a series of branded content campaigns to drive this message home.

This includes the launch of Minecraft bushfire simulation, *Climate Warriors*[2], aimed at educating future generations on how to prepare for natural disasters and *Invisible Fires with Julia Stone*[3], that helped raise awareness for the lasting mental health impacts felt by many post-Australia's Black Summer. In addition to this the brand were behind the feature documentary *A Fire Inside*[4] which has had widespread broadcasting from The Sydney Film Festival, Channel Nine, iTunes, Prime Video and Google Play.

A Fire Inside is a moving documentary that presents the personal tales of those affected by the devastating bushfires in Australia's history. The film features the voices of volunteers, emergency responders, families, friends, and neighbours in communities that were hit by the fires. In addition to the emotional content, smaller, more practical, and socially focused videos have been created to complement the stories and provide individuals with the necessary tools to empower themselves, ultimately leading to heightened brand loyalty. And this consistent dedication to building brand love is also backed up in data.

According to the ranking for 2022, in the 'Brand Finance Australia 100', NRMA achieved a remarkable Brand Strength Index (BSI) score of 84.4 out of 100 and a AAA- brand strength rating, outperforming other insurance brands. This exceptional performance is attributed to the brand's high quality, outstanding reputation, and innovative approach, making NRMA the strongest insurance brand in Australia for 2022.

1 Based on a study performed by Nobel Prize-winning psychologist Daniel Kahneman
2 https://vimeo.com/537595500
3 https://www.youtube.com/watch?v=0NNdoyM-XD0
4 A Fire Inside Trailer - https://www.youtube.com/watch?v=Sn7lRYxNA14

EMILY BULL
The Time Is Right For Branded Video Content

In a world moving to Artificial Intelligence (AI), we need to bring in as much humanity and storytelling to our audiences as we can. Human-to-human storytelling showing emotions, empathy and communication of messages means our audiences can understand connect and respond to the nuances and context in a way that chatbots cannot. And to do this we need time and not to be restricted by 15-second stories. The story should lead the length not the data. Brands may be tempted to prioritise quantity over quality in their content creation due to the demand for constant communication, but this could negatively impact their marketing efforts.

> "The most valuable currency in advertising today is content, not impressions." David Lubars, Chief Creative Officer, BBDO Worldwide, Branded Content Jury Chairman, Cannes LIONS 2021

Brands should be aware of the limitations of bite-sized content and focus on creating meaningful stories that connect with their audiences, instead of just creating content for the sake of the instant gratification of achieving easy numbers. Taking the harder, longer route of brand building through stories and branded content can be an effective way for companies to build stronger relationships with their audiences and ultimately drive brand loyalty, connection, and business growth.

Emily Bull is the Co-Founder and Executive Producer of award-winning branded content agency hellofuture.tv. Emily is a Branded Content Specialist with 20 years industry experience. Beginning her career at Pod Film in Sydney she then spent several years agency side in the UK at Grey London before establishing and running the first film content department at global digital agency AKQA. On her return to Australia, she again established a film content department at The White Agency in Sydney. Emily is a passionate advocate of film content within the digital space. She has been a Cannes Lions Branded Entertainment jury member, and was the Branded Content & Entertainment Jury President at the Spike Asia Awards in 2015. Emily has worked across numerous high profile brands including Bayer, BUPA, Macquarie, P&G, Nokia, Mars, Nike, Fiat, Ferrari, GE, CBA, Xbox, Lexus, VW, Telstra, Diabetes Australia, Ancestry.com.au. Emily is the Head of BCMA Australasia Chapter and a member of the BCMA Global Council.

ADAM SMITH
From Industry to Higher Education: An Influencer Marketing Experiential Learning Programme For Final Year Students

There is little doubt that the development of finely tuned branded content is now a mainstay in marketing across the globe. Organisations large and small are using sophisticated ways to attract new and existing audiences. Social media posts, podcasts, webinars and TikTok videos are just some examples of tools and platforms that have become increasingly popular over the years. However, whilst branded content is not a new phenomenon in industry, it is certainly beginning to yield much interest in higher education.

Marketing employers and recruiters alike are demanding higher-skilled graduates equipped with the readiness for thriving in the cutting-edge world of industry. Students embarking on marketing-related degrees should, thus, expect to be tech-savvy co-creators of branded content as well as possess the customary critical writing and analytical skills to effectively evaluate their own projects and real-life marketing campaigns.

A popular trend in the branded content space, influencer marketing has been around for decades and is now a super force that is expected to grow considerably in the coming years. In simple terms, influencer marketing is used to create exposure to brands, with 'influencers' hired by organisations to produce and share their own content on social media. Whilst there are, as ever, contractual commitments, this is very much a reciprocal arrangement for all parties: influencers are paid for their work, often building followers aligned to their own personal brand, and businesses capitalise on a ready-made target market, using influencers to reach out effectively to consumers with creative content that is unique and innovative.

It is, in my view, at the organisational level where academic institutions are well equipped to teach the underpinnings of bespoke marketing campaigns by creating a culture of real-life experiential learning. Thus, students adopt the role of consultants working on behalf of real clients and are exposed to problems and challenges that reflect the real world. This helps them to develop deep critical thinking skills which can be used to make important strategic decisions; they, too, have strict deadlines to meet and must deliver recommendations that are clear, actionable, and tailored accordingly to their clients' expectations.

ADAM SMITH
From Industry to Higher Education: An Influencer Marketing Experiential Learning Programme For Final Year Students

Providing experiential learning opportunities for students is something that Nottingham Business School (NBS) is passionate about. In 2021, I met Gordon Glenister, the Global Head of Influencer Marketing at the Branded Content Marketing Association (BCMA) and we designed a real-world influencer marketing group assessment for Final Year students.

This was an ambitious project with 20 brands recruited across the UK and more than 400 students working in small teams over a 3-month period. To provide as much practical focus as possible, Gordon delivered two briefing presentations and introduced us to an exclusive online influencer marketing platform called *Influencity*, which students could use to search for profiles of influencers that matched their clients' values and proposed campaigns.

The students had to work together as tight-knit teams to determine a product or service offering and research competitor brands and exemplars in their niche to look at the type of content they wanted to create and the level of engagement. This would help them to develop a clear concept as well as propose social media channels and platforms most suited to their brand. With access to *Influencity* and other research tools, the teams would then try to find the right influencers before preparing an outreach approach (with details of what their influencers should do) and considering ways to measure the success of their campaign.

To round off the project, students delivered 15-minute group presentations to their clients as part of a live showcase event which took place in the Newton building at NBS. There were some excellent and very creative campaigns across the board. Some of the stronger teams provided a clear and detailed critical analysis of the evidence with practical and actionable recommendations that the clients could take away and implement. Even the teams who were graded lower overall academically were still able to demonstrate a thorough understanding of the context as well as provide some good, insightful, and creative ideas. Our influencer marketing assessment was delivered over a two-year period, and we have received some very positive feedback from students, clients, and stakeholders. Overall grades for the module have also increased from 78% of 2:1s and above in the 2020/21 academic year to 84% last year, which is a clear indication of where our learning outcomes align closely to the assessment and how such a relevant and hugely popular topic was a good fit all round.

ADAM SMITH
From Industry to Higher Education: An Influencer Marketing Experiential Learning Programme For Final Year Students

Some students have also been offered exciting internship opportunities with their clients and all students received certificates of completion from the BCMA.

Nottingham Trent University students and their Influencer Marketing presentation

Whilst it was a challenging large-scale operation, it was extremely rewarding to see the students share ideas and develop crucial employability skills which can be used in numerous organisations and sectors. Working with Gordon and the BCMA has also had a significant impact on the students' understanding of influencer marketing and the broader practical challenges of delivering branded content as part of a live experiential learning programme.

Adam Smith is Principal Lecturer and Programme Leader at Nottingham Business School which is part of Nottingham Trent University. He is an experienced Business Adviser, Mentor and Chartered Member of the CMI with over 10-years of teaching and academic management experience in Higher Education. He has been an Executive In-Company Development Mentor for corporate degree apprenticeship students and has supervised consultancy projects at postgraduate level for clients including East Midlands Waterways, Experian UK & Ireland, 3M Health Care, Flower Pod, Pukka Pedals and the Nottinghamshire Wildlife Trust. Adam is an aspiring professional with keen educational interests, and continues to develop his broadening portfolio. He holds a Master's degree in Business & Management Research from Loughborough University and is a Fellow of the Higher Education Academy. In 2016, he also completed a postgraduate Level 7 Diploma in Professional Consulting with the CMI.

CRISTIAN LIARTE
Branded Content Evolution: Brand Influence

Beyond the ins and outs of the evolution of Branded Content and its impact and influence on broadcasters and publishers, we see clearly how the brand influence on the digital ecosystem and consumption is increasing whether the audiences are aware of and perceive it or not.

With many players having brand-funded programming on Rakuten TV, we couldn't take advantage of this opportunity, even more being an AVOD platform where advertisers are critical for our business model.

Recent research shows that display advertising is rapidly losing its effectiveness due to the widespread use of ad-blocking software, and viewers tend to ignore explicit commercials. So that's the opportunity to explain stories from the Brand side without a prominent commercial sense.

Considering your audience as authentic individuals instead of simply 'customers', with brand content initiatives, you can foster relationships emotionally with your audience through engaging stories and content rather than explicit advertising.

Rakuten TV is a great example of how a brand can interact with audiences in different layers, whether co-producing content, sponsoring them, within the stories with product placement, and enjoying the business with the best media plans, coverages, and returns on the investment building a model cost-effective than a regular campaign. And on top of a massive European coverage in 42 countries in Europe and 150 million households or locally segmented.

Cristian Liarte is the Head of Originals at Rakuten TV. He has 20-year's experience and is passionate and curious about all aspects of media entertainment, from production to scriptwriting, content sales, operations and finance. Cristian has worked for companies including Grupo Secuoya, Endemol, La Fábrica de la Tele, and Mediapro. He was Executive Producer and Chief Operating Officer at the award-winning company El Cañonazo Transmedia the full-service production company specialising in content creation.

PATRICK LINDON
The Year Of Influencer Marketing... I Mean Rabbit

Is 2023 FINALLY the year of Influencer Marketing? Throughout the late noughties and early 10s the marketing and advertising industry was adamant, every January, to claim this year is the year of the mobile. Exactly what event we were expecting to occur to declare it the Year of The Mobile no one can say. At best, one could make a case for 2013, when smartphone sales surpassed 'traditional' phones. There is some poetic justice here in that the years of playing snake on your Nokia 3310 were finished in the year of the Snake. Suffice it to say, it didn't happen in a specific year, in fact, the mobile industry constantly evolved with key milestones along the way.

This is where influencer marketing (or the Creator Economy if you want to avoid negative connotations derived from media coverage) is arriving in 2023. The question is no longer whether to run influencer marketing campaigns, but instead the questions are about lower funnel metric measurement, Niche or Macro creators, or how long and how often should we be active. However, while it might not be the year, it is a year where we will see an overall market shift into practices that help drive consumers down the funnel, create more brand advocates, and is no longer a 'bolt-on' extension to a social element of the campaign.

There are three key elements that will be key indicators of the maturity of influencer marketing.

1. An increase in the non-traditional media platforms becoming involved in the creator economy: Recently, Amazon announced they are exploring ways to leverage its app and create its own influencer-style content offering within it. This creates an interesting dynamic in this space with non-traditional content hosting platforms now leveraging their current customer base. For many years, the path to purchase on a mobile device was 'clunky' and did not incentivise consumers to leave the platform to purchase; cue in-app shop pages. This created a natural barrier as it is a heavy lift for many smaller brands to create and maintain their social platform-specific shop page. Instead, ensuring your product is available on Amazon and you are working with creators to review and promote your product within an app has strong appeal to those focused on ROI and ROAS.

PATRICK LINDON
The Year Of Influencer Marketing...I Mean Rabbit

A seamless experience such as this would lead to the eventual demise of the 'Link in Bio' plug.

Obviously, this is not the way it is all going to go, but it is an interesting way to think about how there are other platforms that can encourage creators into their ecosystem, or provide the current audience with more personalised and entertaining information or infotainment

As an aside to this, it will not be long until LinkedIn is offering a video conference feature to expedite job interviews and offer an easier way to solidify connections.

2. Refocusing on Micro and Nano creators to be leveraged with Paid Social: While many brands and marketers are still buying based on creator audience size, there is an observable shift to the desire to work with creators who have a smaller niche audience. These audiences provide access to content creation and reaching audiences at lower costs and a way to test different audience types and content formats. With more and more brands looking for long-term collaborations, this is a great way in finding the talent to be part of their growth journey and establish high levels of trust with them and their audience. Investing in homegrown authentic creators is something the creator, brand, and audience all want. Authentic content presented in the tone and voice known to that creator is relatable and even if paid for by *'brand X'* is an acceptable value exchange to all parties. Platforms are altering the algorithm that rewards people based on the DNA of the content and not necessarily their size.

The second and arguably more important part of this is that it is vital for brands to layer Paid Social on top of the organic work. I believe there are two reasons for this:

> 1) The platforms are savvy to the money that is not going into their pockets as it is passing from brand to creator, so they are creating a 'Pay to Play' space. This is based on what has been seen with organic post performance on like-for-like content that is left to run organically against those that have paid behind it.

> 2) Lower funnel metrics and guaranteed exposure to the desired audience: The organic element is a real-world test of how people are responding to the content.

However, the paid promotion allows you to test and learn what works and does not work: Images, Video, Funny, Music, no Music, etc. Learning how to drive those further metrics and shift a campaign from just awareness to preference and desire. But be mindful that the KPIs of organic content and Paid Social must be separated.

3. An Always On-Approach to Influencer Marketing: As the marketing landscape continues to evolve, it's clear that influencer marketing is not just a trend – it is a strategy that's here to stay. However, to truly maximise the benefits of influencer marketing, it's important to have an always-on strategy in place. Rather than simply launching campaigns periodically, the always-on approach means that you're consistently partnering with the same or new influencers promoting your brand, products, or services. This can involve a mix of sponsored posts, collaborations, brand ambassador programs, and more. With this, you can build stronger relationships with influencers over time because you're not just reaching out to them when you have a specific campaign or product launch in mind – you're consistently engaging with them and working together on a variety of projects. This allows influencers to get to know your brand better, and vice versa resulting in better content and better overall results.

This strategy helps to maintain a consistent brand message across all your influencer partnerships and leverage larger activations for key events or seasonal moments across the year. This can help to establish your brand identity, build brand awareness, and create a stronger connection with your target audience. The increase in content and creators allows for ongoing data analysis and optimisation. Brands can track and analyse data over time, including engagement rates, conversions, and customer sentiment, and can adjust their messaging, products, and services to better resonate with their target audience and improve their ROI.

BONUS: A bonus to this will be a boom in brands and creators collaborating more to launch their own products in the DTC e-commerce market. Looking at the success of the PRIME drink launch and similar ventures with creators who are not as world-known shows brands that consumers might be more loyal to influencers than to a corporation's product. People do not mind being sold to, it is who, when, and how they are spoken to that can invite action. Allowing a path for different revenue streams for content creators is ideal and reduces their dependency on one (or several) platforms that are continually evolving and changing to compete with each other.

PATRICK LINDON
The Year Of Influencer Marketing...I Mean Rabbit

Each platform is just one algorithm shift away from potentially making their content move from desirable to invisible (intentionally or not).

One could argue that you could roll all three of these ideas into one big trend. What is being observed is the purchase funnel becoming more of a loop with a full-funnel approach to creator marketing (see image below). The barrier from being a consumer learning about a product from your favourite creators to an active brand advocate is just the upload of a single TikTok video away (with a few @ mentions and a clever dance).

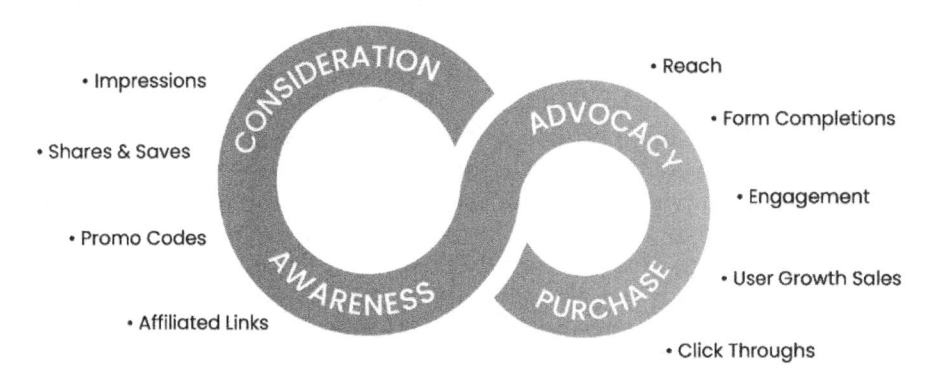

Credit: Open Influence Marketing team

A fear with waiting for the Year of the Mobile is that by the time it was realised it had most likely happened, we had already moved on to the next big thing and new expectations. While there is likely not to be a Year of the Influencer, it is a year where brands will double down on ensuring it has their own item line on a marketing plan and is no longer an asterisk on the social media line.

Maybe we should take a page from the Chinese Zodiac signs and the traits associated with the year of the Rabbit: *affectionate people who excel at forming close relationships*...sounds similar to those nano and micro-influencers to me.

Patrick Lindon is the UK Senior Sales Manager at Open Influence and Director of Education for BCMA Influence. Open Influence is a full-service company that works with brands by matching them with the right influencers across all platforms including Snapchat, Instagram, Twitter, Facebook, TikTok and YouTube to tell their brand story.

BRUCE BILDSTEN
BMW Films: Perfect Mini Movies

Ask most people when modern branded content was born, and they'll likely say 2001 with BMW Films. I was fortunate enough to be there for the conception, labour, birth and even first steps of this groundbreaking work.

BMW Films - the formal title was *The Hire* - were eight short films, designed to be experienced only online, introduced in two seasons. They starred the then relatively unknown Clive Owen as an enigmatic driver for hire who naturally chose a BMW for his work. It was the brainchild of my ad agency, Fallon, where I was the creative lead on the BMW account and was only made possible by some very brave and forward-thinking clients at BMW North America led by Marketing VP, Jim McDowell.

The films were treated like "perfect mini movies" (to quote a famous film critic when they were released), with top Hollywood talent both behind and in front of the camera.

Season One was executive produced by David Fincher and Season Two by Tony and Ridley Scott. Each was a unique stand-alone film with Clive the connecting tissue, all under ten minutes long, helmed by a who's who of top Hollywood and Oscar-winning directors: John Frankenheimer, Ang Lee, Guy Ritchie, Wong Kar Wai, Alejandro Innuritu, John Woo, Joe Carnahan, and Tony Scott. They featured an equally star-studded cast, including Madonna, Mickey Rourke, Forest Whitaker, Stellan Skarsgård, Don Cheadle, Gary Oldman, and James Brown. But it didn't end there: The very best editors, colourists, sound designers, composers, and stunt coordinators were enlisted as well.

It began, like so many great creative solutions, with a business problem. BMW had realized that TV advertising wasn't the most effective way to reach their affluent, active buyers. Their buyers weren't sitting home, watching TV: They were skiing, playing tennis, visiting vineyards, living life. At the same time, we knew that their buyers were using this new thing called the Internet to do everything from check their stocks to shop for cars. BMW and our team at Fallon had long lamented that a thirty-second television commercial couldn't begin to capture the breath taking performance of a BMW.

BRUCE BILDSTEN
BMW Films: Perfect Mini Movies

In fact, we collectively watched classic car chases featuring BMWs, like John Frankenheimer's classic chase through Paris in *Ronin* and thought "if only our commercials could feel like that".

Finally, it was time to do something about it. McDowell and his team wrote us a letter, challenging us to come back to them with something bigger than a 30-second commercial to solve this problem. Talk about laying down the gauntlet.

Back at Fallon a creative team working on BMW - David Carter and the late Joe Sweet - had just finished a long-form commercial for Timex Watches with Tim Burton. It had given them a taste of what's possible when a commercial was not approached like a commercial. They took the challenge from our clients and literally laid the big idea on my lap: An action film featuring a BMW that would be delivered in short segments, only on the internet. It took us fifteen minutes to present the idea to Jim and his team at BMW and about fifteen seconds for them to say "yes", with some considerable caveats. We'd have to prove that we could attract top Hollywood talent, we'd need to help him build a compelling business case, and we'd need to figure out a technological solution to deliver the content on the circa 2001 Worldwide Web.

Let's start with the last challenge. It was several years before the invention of YouTube and the widespread availability of high-speed internet. But our crack technical team at Fallon was up to the challenge. In essence, we created our own YouTube called 'The BMW Films Player' using an early version of Apple's QuickTime platform. There still was the internet bandwidth issue: But we were confident that anxious fans would patiently download them overnight.

Next was the talent issue. We honestly had little concern about that. In the early 2000's Fallon was arguably one of the hottest creative agencies in the world with an unofficial internal motto of 'go big or go home'. Our fearless producers immediately picked up the phone and had conversations with the like of Martin Scorsese and John Frankenheimer. Ultimately, the late (and great) producer Steve Golin of Anonymous Content and his partner David Fincher took on the challenge. It was Fincher who suggested moving from one film delivered in chapters to a series of unique individual films. He argued, correctly, that we could attract top talent if we could limit a director's commitment to as little as six or eight weeks, making it easier to fit a film into their feature film schedules. There was another advantage to individual films, which Jim McDowell dubbed 'the mutual fund effect'.

BRUCE BILDSTEN
BMW Films: Perfect Mini Movies

In short, we'd spread our risk out over five films to get the formula absolutely right.

While the level of talent and production values may look lavish, every penny invested was scrutinised. (There is no bean counter more devoted than a German bean counter!) Jim was determined not to spend a penny more than his quarterly brand campaign budget. Rather, the production to media ratios were reversed: A small promotional budget along with a tremendous buzz led viewers online where the media was essentially free.

Finally, there was the challenge to build help the BMW marketing team build the business case. This subject alone could take another chapter, but I'll simplify it here. Some very bright minds on the Fallon account team, devised a measurement they called the 'brand minute'. In essence it was a metric that compared the cost of a film, where a customer would be deeply engaged in our brand for seven minutes, with that of a traditional television media buy, where you might be lucky enough to capture their fleeting attention for thirty seconds. We projected that the cost of that attention would be lower with the online films. Ultimately turned out to be dramatically lower.

So, the business case was made, the best talent was engaged, and the technological hurdles were cleared. But what was it that ultimately made the resulting films so compelling? Simply put, it was BMW's promise to let the filmmakers make films. The car was simply another character in the film. They were never modified to perform better on screen. If anything, the heavy camera rigs restrained the car's performance. The BMWs were crashed, shot up, and cloaked in dust. There were no gratuitous close-ups of features and no badge shots. If you expected people to seek you out online - especially in 2001- and download a film overnight to view it, it damn better be worth it.

Jim and his team were brave in yet another way: They knew within an intensely sales-driven organisation like BMW that spending millions of dollars on film production would sound lavish if not reckless. So, as we developed the concept and started production the BMW team kept the project largely secret within their walls, after getting approval from the North American and global CEO's. Jim and his team knew that a few dissenting voices could doom the project from the beginning. They also knew that if it didn't work, they may well be looking for another job and their agency would be looking for another automotive client. I distinctly remember presenting the idea to BMW North America CEO, Tom Purves with McDowell at the hospitality tent of a Formula 1™ race.

BRUCE BILDSTEN
BMW Films: Perfect Mini Movies

He understood its potential, but cautiously added "This is either going to be a huge success or no one will notice."

But people did notice and quickly. We think it might have been a DVD that was surreptitiously sent to Vanity Fair editor Graydon Carter that started the underground buzz. Impressed, he shared it with some other media friends, and suddenly critics for the two most influential publications of the time, The New York Times and Time Magazine, had run stories singing the film's praises. The word was out: You just have to see them. The films were released one at a time, spread weeks apart as we completed production. We hadn't even lined up directors and actors for the later films, but Frankenheimer's film was first, and when other directors saw what the king of the car chase had created, they wanted in.

The buzz was everywhere, with the films attracting film buffs and car fanatics in equal measure. And they were remarkably successful in the marketplace. BMWs had always been cool, but now they were Clive Owen cool. BMW Films became a Harvard Business School Case Study. I stopped counting how many people told me they learned about the films in business school.

Of course, the films won every top advertising award, even though they weren't traditional advertising. The Cannes Lions even went as far to create a new top award, The Titanium Lion 'for work that makes people stop in their tracks and consider the way forward'. They influenced scores of young filmmakers - including Neil Blomkamp who directed the fifteenth anniversary film *The Escape* for us in 2016 - and fanboys still sing their praises on social media.

I might be biased, but twenty years later I still don't think there is a piece of branded content that surpasses their quality and impact. And that's because they weren't BMW Commercials. They were BMW Films, in every sense of the word.

Bruce Bildsten is the Executive Creative Director at Best Buy. Bruce spent over twenty-five years as a copywriter and creative director at Fallon. He led brands like BMW, PBS, United Airlines, and Cadillac, while helping to build one of the world's most award-winning creative departments. He was the leader of the team that created the groundbreaking BMW Films branded content series.

ACKNOWLEDGMENTS

First and foremost, we would like to thank everyone who contributed their thoughts and shared their expert opinions, namely, Sir John Hegarty, Professor Jonathan Hardy, Dr. Helen Powell, Maya Bogle, Gordon Glenister, Simon Orpin, Jeanette Okwu, Simon Bell, Shannon Walker, Spero Patricios, Lawrence Ribero, Karnvir Mundrey, Dr. Sevil Yesiloglu, Haem Roy, Daniel Sánchez, Álvaro Bermúdez de Castro, Adam Kaczmarski, Professor Iain Macrury, Silvia Velasco Praga, Olgierd Cygan, Mariana Lorena, Armando Díaz, Chantal Rickards OBE, Greg Turzynski, Jo Farmer, Geraint Lloyd-Taylor, Alan Hunt, Emily Stirling, Nina Glynn, Melanie Loeper, Megan Tandy, Stefano Marrone, Sandra Freisinger-Heinl, Christina Kufer, Patricia Weiss, James Hayr, Sandra Lehner, Martin Laing, Tom Higgins, Dr Tauheed A. Ramjaun, Monique Centrone PhD, Rick Parkhill, Sylvia Enotiades, Jessica Millowick, Dr Rula Al Abdulrazak, Rebecca Allen, Julie Dardour, Adam Harris, Katherine Elizabeth Ekrami, Emily Bull, Adam Smith, Cristian Liarte, Patrick Lindon, Bruce Bildsten.

With particular thanks to Greg Turzynski for his editorial skills, expert advice and unwavering support.

A special thank you to Phil DiIanni at BMW North America for the permission to use the imagery on the front and back cover from the latest BMW Film series, The Escape. Last but by no means least, thank you to all our BCMA 'Family' - Chapter Heads, Affiliate Partners and Members for their incredible support.

We look forward with great anticipation and excitement to the next twenty years.

ABOUT THE AUTHOR

Andrew Canter is amongst the leading global practitioners in branded content and has thirty years experience working in marketing communications.

He is the Global CEO of the Branded Content Marketing Association (BCMA), the leading worldwide body for branded content practitioners, promoting best practice, sharing knowledge and growing the branded content industry.

He has been instrumental in developing the global content monitoring evaluation system measuring the effectiveness of branded content and influencer marketing campaigns.

He is responsible for spearheading the development of BCMA chapters spanning the globe, from the USA to India and pretty much everywhere in between.

Andrew is Honorary Professor at the School of Arts and Digital Industries, University of East London – the first Professor of Branded Content and has taught at the Met Film School. He is co-author of the academic study, *Defining Branded Content For The Digital Age* and several other publications, including Fifteen Years, A Branded Content Story, bringing together 60 leading industry experts.

Andrew lectures in Branded Content Marketing and regularly speaks at international conferences and has been on many international award judging panels. He is an Advisor to the Branded Content Research Network that brings together leading Academics and Practitioners.

Andrew is married with three young children. He has supported Watford Football Club for almost fifty years and is a passionate collector of all things horological. He's a Liveryman in the Worshipful Company of Clockmakers and has been awarded the Freedom of the City of London. Andrew is a volunteer tour guide at the Clockmaker's Museum, the world's oldest collection of clocks and watches housed at the Science Museum in South Kensington. He is Co-Founder of MrWatchMaster, a marketing platform to 'talk about watches'.

BRANDED CONTENT MARKETING ASSOCIATION (BCMA)

The Branded Content Marketing Association (BCMA) is the leading global member association for branded content and influencer marketing.

The BCMA promotes the value of branded content and is designed for anyone involved in the communications industry.

Through best practice it leads the debate on what makes great branded content and how brands, producers, platforms and agencies can engage audiences for maximum benefit and payback.

BCMA commissions research, measures effectiveness, offers strategic advice and hosts events about the branded content and influencer marketing industries. It creates the opportunity to connect with the leading experts in branded content and influencer marketing.

With extensive reach offering a unique global industry perspective, BCMA Chapters now operate in multiple markets stretching from North America to India. BCMA launched the *Branded Content Research Hub*, in partnership with the University of the Arts London (UAL) and builds a 'bridge' between Academia and Industry teaching the requisite skills required for branded content and influencer marketing practitioners.

To mark the BCMA's landmark twenty-year anniversary, it has brought together the branded content and influencer marketing industry's leading experts with a collection of inspiring, thought-provoking and engaging essays.

They share their incredible stories and insights into how branded content and influencer marketing has evolved and come to the forefront of marketing communications and how it will continue to shape the future of advertising and communications industry.

For more information, please visit www.thebcma.info

DISCLAIMER

This book is designed to provide information and motivation to our readers. It is sold with the understanding that the publisher is not engaged to render any type of psychological, legal, or any other kind of professional advice. The content is the sole expression and opinion of its contributors, and not necessarily that of the author, publisher or anyone associated with the Branded Content Marketing Association (BCMA). No warranties or guarantees are expressed or implied by the publisher's choice to include any of the content in this volume. Neither the publisher nor the individual author(s) shall be liable for any physical, psychological, emotional, financial, or commercial damages, including, but not limited to, special, incidental, consequential or other damages. Our views and rights are the same: You are responsible for your own choices, actions, and results.

NOTES

Printed in Great Britain
by Amazon